popeye never told you

Novels by Rodney Hall

The Ship on the Coin

A Place Among People

Just Relations

Kisses of the Enemy

Captivity Captive

The Second Bridegroom

The Grisly Wife

The Yandilli Trilogy / A Dream More Luminous that Love

The Island in the Mind

The Day we had Hitler Home

The Last Love Story

Love without Hope

RODNEY HALL

popeye never told you

childhood memories of the war

PIER 9

for Michael and Diana

The shop door opens and the little bell jingles, but Mum tells me not to touch that white woolly thing folded on the shelf,

not to touch anything,

a woman reaches up to open my bedroom curtains and shes got a big white X on her back, i watch her and i know her and when i am five i shall know everything.

5

Mike heaves the window down to slam it shut, and Di comes running across the carpet just in time to see the *whole town* change into black chimneys and glass flashes and this one *WOW!* comes so close i duck and the windows rattle and i see weird rooms over there like bright toilets and rooms with cupboards and enormous shadows flicker on the wallpaper, but im not afraid because Mikes here and im going to be a sailor anyway! and a puff of smoke drifts past in front of everything but i press my nose against the mesh,

'*BKHHHURR!*' i shout back at the explosion,

and the din is terrific with the air raid sirens wailing as well,

'lets get out of here!' Di says,

'but we shall miss the *smoke!*' i say,

and i ought to rescue Teddy from the bedroom but ive got to keep watch, and the noise is all around though you cant tell if its coming or going and bits of stuff come flying past out of the dark and im thirsty,

'look at those searchlights' Mike says,

so i crane my neck,

'—moment to lose!' Mums voice suddenly screams,

and shes like a ghost in the doorway!

and Mike springs down and gets busy because we all know what to do, and Di tugs at the black-out curtains to pin them together so theres not even a crack left,

and now Mike gives me a push 'move!' he says,

and i hate that so i hit him and i wish i could hit harder but hes too big,

'get *off* the settee' he says,

but the gasmask dangling round my neck strangles me and my tin helmet slips crooked,

'okay' Mike says while he dashes about, beginning to push the settee all by himself 'now roll it!'

and Di helps trundle the big thing across the carpet till its back clunks up against the piano to make a safety tunnel because the piano is the biggest thing in our flat standing up against the wall, and i know this is the drill we practised but all i do is watch, though im still the first to dive into the tunnel because im the littlest, so now when the roof falls in we can be safe,

'super!'

and i wriggle right along to the end and crouch there,

and Di gets in next,

'your teeth are chattering' she says,

'no theyre not'

and even under here i can see a flash of torchlight

because Mums still moving around the room outside our tunnel,

'listen to this' Mike says,

and with both hands together he presses down on the loud pedal and i can hear *humming* inside the piano,

'hurry up, Mum' i yell,

'hurry up, Mum!' Di yells,

because the enemy planes make the whole place shake, so i think its best to count to ten and i bet if theres not another bomb before ten we wont be hit and this could be the end of the war,

at last Mum crawls in with us and shes bringing a flat tin,

'whats that?' Mike asks,

'old snapshots of our farm in Australia' Mum says,

'you never told us about that' i say,

so Mikes first with it because hes down that end and she gives him the pencil-torch so he can look okay and i watch him looking at a photograph and his eyes glow in the torchlight,

but theres a BANG so big it makes me jump and i hit my head, and Dianas got the photo and the torch so she shares with me,

'can you see this, Rod?'

but i cant because of my eyes,

'heres a pointy rock' Di says,

i cant,

‘and heres a lady’ Di shows me and she kisses me,

‘thats me’ says Mum ‘when i was young’

so i rub my tears on my sleeve and i can see her there in riding breeches and shes reaching up to touch the tip of the rock,

‘and thats not a rock, its an ant-hill’ Mum says ‘back at home’

but *this* is home, this flat where we live,

‘you find them all over the place’ she says ‘so i chose the biggest’

and its so enormous it must be full of ants as big as dogs! then why wasnt she running?

another bomb goes off,

‘*that* shook the foundations’ Mike says,

‘heres a snap of our road’ Mum says ‘from the farm to town’

‘can you see the road, Rod?’ Di asks and she shares so we can look together,

‘and heres a horse’ she shows me,

‘his name was George’ says Mum,

‘and heres a cart’ says Di,

and i love her so i blink and i blink and i try to see,

‘the cart’ Di tells me about it ‘is half way up the hill’

but i still cant make it out and everything in our flat is shaking and rattling,

the fishmongers wife scrubs her stone slab with a brush and sloshes water on it and im allowed to watch,

'was your dad killed in the war then?' she asks,
but i hate it when people ask,
the slab flashes in the sun and i make up my mind,
'yes he was' i lie,
and she sloshes some more,

i want you to know because im thinking about you all the time,

but the street outside is quiet and the whole towns empty because its Sunday and the shop blinds stay down and church bells are donging, and we sit around playing favourites while we wait for Mum to get up now that shes had her cup of tea, like whats your favourite book and whats your favourite card game, and i have a favourite *name* that i keep secret and nobody will ever guess in a thousand years, and we dont have to go shopping today because the shops arent open,

'darlings?' Mum calls from the bedroom in a little voice 'somebody?'

and im the one who goes in, while Diana and Michael wait behind for me to bring them the lastest news, and shes lying on top of the bed and the blue bedspread is all shiny around her and underneath her and shes put some pillows in a stack for her head to go on, and shes got one hand on her head and her arms white and she gives me an empty glass with the other hand, so i take it back into the kitchen,

'she still has her headache from the *overtime*' i say 'and its really bad'

so i get busy filling the glass with water for her and Mike fetches the Anadins from the cupboard because hes the oldest and Di pours her a fresh cup of tea, but the Anadins are the main thing and they can never be taken by children because the pills come in a tiny tin thats a special green colour,

we play hands-knees-and-bumps-a-daisy, and Diana and i bump our bottoms and this is so funny we fall over and bottom is a naughty word, and Gran says we can have as many apricots as we like so im up on the step ladder and im pulling them off her tree to stuff them in my mouth and theyre so squishy the juice runs down my chin,

'you greedy thing' Gran says and shes laughing at me 'careful you dont swallow the stone as well!'

'because why?'

'because then i should think an apricot tree will grow inside you'

so i think about that and Di looks at me like she can see it happening already.

'*then* what?' i say,

'then youll sprout leaves out of your mouth and nose' and Gran laughs till she shakes all over because shes fat and old,

but its only a goods train passing because the rumble lasts such a long time and im awake in bed so i reach out to lift a corner of the black-out curtain and let in some moonlight but theres nothing in our room except Mike on his bed and the cupboard in the corner, and i shall be ready when the air raid sirens start up and im going to bolt for the lounge room to help push the settee,

but everythings quiet and all there is is our kitchen clock ticking,

i let the curtain drop,

but the dark is worse because now i cant help thinking, and what i think about is enemy commandos and parachutes floating down into a field that looks like the field where Mum takes us picking mushrooms, so i lift the curtain again and look out at the empty yard and i hold it up till my arm gets tired and i have to boggle my eyes,

the first cross-over for the knot is easy because Mike shows me how, so i loop one lace and now i wind the other around and through, and this looks good! i give it a pull, but the *whole thing* falls apart so i tug my shoes off and chuck them across the room,

'lets try again' Mike says,

and the railway is where everything happens and im a good train-spotter because we are always spotting and the tracks pass just down the back of our place and we can play in the coal bunkers, and the rain doesnt matter,

even Diana knows about trains although shes a girl,

and this rusty siding isnt used anymore and these stones are called clinkers, and i hunch my shoulders and give the peak of my cap a good tug and the rain patters on my mackintosh and wet weeds brush my knees and drops get caught in my eyelashes, but i keep walking and watching my shoes crunch the clinkers and when i look back Mike and Di are still under that leaky roof of the old goods platform where we go because its the best place for spotting when the express trains rush through,

but they catch up at the coal bunkers so we hang around together and jump in for a soft landing because the coal dust is thick and squidgy and we jump till drips get down the back of my collar and i dont *like* it, so im going home and once we get there im going to stop indoors and play with our model railway even though the lines get pulled apart and bent and this always leads to quarrels,

and the blasted rain gets heavier and heavier and im sick of it and therell be puddles outside and water running down the wall because of the leaky gutter Mum cant fix, but what i like is our big back yard is up on the roof of the garage, because thats what the yard is, and i can lean over the skylights to look down where the mechanics are fixing cars,

and when the weathers nice we scramble up on the flat roof of our kitchen too, so thats what we do in summer because this is where we hide the junket we make and we squat down on the kitchen roof to eat it, and i love junket though Mum thinks its disgusting and its usually okay except for a few flecks of soot, and we dont even argue and we take our shirts off to get some sun, but last time Michael told Diana she should keep hers on because shes a girl, and i know the difference between boys and girls of course but i couldnt see what showing her chest had to do with it,

but now im in a temper because i cant find *anything* in this blasted cupboard so i begin throwing junk out all over the floor and i wont give in, not even if i have to *wreck everything*,

i stand back while i watch the blind man feel his way into our flat going straight to the piano and then taking the front off it,

'did you know it can hum all by itself?' i ask him,

and theres lots of strings inside,

'no, i didnt know that' he says, but he misses me with his look,

and he gets busy and i can tell how the tunings going because i watch his face pinch up till it comes right,

and Mum says our piano is a good one, but the tuner cant read the brass alphabet *Schreiber* because his eyes dont work like mine,

and anyway i run to the window because Mikes begun the game of spitting down on the cars that turn in underneath us when they come to fill up with petrol, and when they drive out again you get a second go, but you have to lean right over the sill if you want a good shot at them,

'youre too little for spitting' Mike says,

but i spit like a champion,

and if no cars come i aim at peoples hats instead,

the window i like best is Mums bedroom because Mike and Di like the lounge and so i can have it to myself and all three of us can hang out together and count one two three *spit!* at the same time,

'dont fall!' Mike says,

and i hit a black umbrella, super!

and Mums bedroom smells nice because on the dressing-table theres a squirter with a tassel and her double bed is covered with a bedspread made of silk and thats where Diana sleeps too because she doesnt have a bed of her own, but ive got my own bed thats under the window in our room and Mikes got a bed too over by the wall, but our window is no good for spitting from because its at the back and theres nothing below, only the yard you can climb out on to,

so i walk right up close behind Mum and we are on this grassy hill *striding* along in the wet with me being the copycat planting my feet where she plants hers and i trudge across the common right up to the fort just one step behind her, but she never once turns round to catch me out because she knows this game,

'you are welcome in my kingdom' says Mike,

he got here first but theres nothing to see except

the view with fields and a whole lot of barrage balloons floating in the rain above the town,

'so many balloons!' Diana says,

'theyre to stop low-flying aeroplanes' Mike explains,

'how?' i say and i dont think they could stop anything because i know that balloons only *burst*,

'some day' says Mum 'you must ask your Uncle Ralph about them'

'he *never* comes to see us' Di says 'we havent got any uncles'

'he never does' i say too 'and we dont even *know* him'

and i skip ahead with Diana so we can sing together,

'we love the war!' we sing 'we love the war!'

but Michael wont join in because he thinks hes too grown up and he holds on to Mums elbow when her high heels skid in the squelch,

my socks keep slipping down around my ankles and they bother me the whole time, but when i fell over my knees got grazed and Gran calls the scabs that i like picking my *war wounds*,

every week the paper shop gets in new stuff so we go there to look at the comics though we cant afford them, but i know my ABC so i read the short bits like *Ow!* and *Ouch!* and there are Meddlesome Mattie comics and Beano comics, and my favourite is Popeye because Popeye wont put up with it and he smokes a pipe and he has a tattoo and hes stronger than anybody and bashes them and thats what im going to be like, and even Gran says Popeye sets a good example because he eats up his vegetables, but all Popeye ever eats is spinach and the trouble is that Gran means turnips and swedes as well,

so Mum stands with us on the footpath while an amazing black car flashes in the sun and comes to a stop, and Uncle Dick Riney steps out though we never saw him before in our lives and hes not a proper uncle anyway, but Mums told us all about him and hes all buttoned up for goodness sake! and Aunt Miriams wrapped in fur and she kisses us and i can smell her perfume sticking to me,

'so this is where you live, Dods!' says Uncle Dick and he strides about here and there in the street getting a squiz,

and i look round too though theres nothing to see,

and we already know that Uncle Dick is a Big Noise because he owns a bus company, but i reckon he should be away at the war with everyone fighting to save us from Hitler,

'Jeremy!' Aunt Mirrie calls and theres a kid on the back seat 'Jeremy do come out and meet Aunty Dods and the children'

and i love this car more than anything i ever loved before because theres rows of silver screws along the bonnet that i can reach if i lean against the mudguard and i let my fingers touch them and this car is the most *gorgeous* thing in the whole world,

'shes a handmade Railton Special' says Uncle Dick pulling me away,

and a whole lot of grown-ups stop to look and a boy on a scooter falls off because hes staring so much and hes someone i know and i stand close to the car when i give him a wave,

'we had an air raid' i tell Uncle Dick,

'Jeremy!' Jeremys mother calls,

at last the door opens and a kid steps out on the runningboard and he jumps down to the pavement on both feet,

'*there* you are!' says his mother,

our new uncle smiles at us showing his gold teeth, and i smile at him because ive been waiting all my life for a car ride, 'may i sit in the drivers seat?' i ask 'so i can have a go at the wheel?'

but Aunt Mirrie laughs at me and then Jeremy joins in and Uncle Dick shakes his head and looks amazed and says 'what? in those grubby pants!'

and someone takes my hand and its Mum,

but im not giving in so i ask 'whats its top speed?'

'a hundred and forty mph' says Uncle Dick and he pats my head,

'this ones a bright spark, Dods!' he says,

but as soon as Diana sits on the runningboard he hoists her up by one arm, and he kisses her and then he locks his car with a silver key,

'well weve arrived at last' says Uncle Dick 'so where do we go?'

but already hes leading the way across the street while we follow behind and dawdle down along our back lane, kicking at scraps of garbage,

'youre not to be shocked' Mum tells them,

and while she shows the Rineys up our back stairs she keeps knocking the corrugated iron wall with her knuckles, and all at once we get to the top,

'thats the back door to our flat' Mike says, pointing across the yard,

so they stand puffing and getting a good look,

'its the *only* door' i say,

and at last we have some real visitors who settle in

the comfortable chairs and they start telling Mum how pleased they are,

'this little flat is so snug!' says Aunt Mirrie,

'and its been such a fine spring day for motoring' says Uncle Dick,

'and we are so very pleased, Dods' Aunt Mirrie says 'to hear about your job with the Ministry of Food'

'better than that babywear shop you had' Uncle Dick says,

'though im sure it was a beautiful shop' Aunt Mirrie says,

'yes but a job is more solid' Uncle Dick tells her,

and Mum brings lunch on plates for everyone to put on their laps,

and i pull a face at Jeremy while hes munching,

'and as for you, little man' Aunt Mirrie says to me as if im her favourite already 'you remind me of your dear father' and she pinches hold of my cheek and waggles it so i feel stupid and she speaks in a loud voice 'what do you say to that?'

and i say 'i dont remem—'

'his father was so handsome' she tells us all 'my Dick used to be quite green with jealousy, werent you, pet?'

and Uncle Dick gives her a wink though Mum says winking is vulgar,

and Jeremy sprawls on the settee while he watches his mother and father cracking jokes, but i spy Mike nudging Di in the ribs now weve finished so we all slip out together to get away, along the corridor we go where we cant be seen and run through the kitchen and out into the yard where we climb up on the roof and Mike and i explode with laughter because nobody will find us here and Diana bursts into tears,

'i *hate* those people' she says,

so i give her my hanky because shes upset and now she can blow her nose too,

'i want to *poison* them!' she says,

'cheer up' Michael says 'its not hard to get poison because quite ordinary things are poisonous, like pear pips'

'pear pips!' i yell at him because that's so *ridiculous*,

but Mike sticks his nose in the air 'its scientific' he says 'theres cyanide in pear pips'

and i know cyanide is the same as arsenic, but Di still has her doubts,

'so how do we get the Rineys to eat them?' she asks,

Mike says 'we can if its just Jeremy because we dont have to persuade Jeremy, we force him'

and i feel better now,

but when Mum calls us Michael climbs down to go in and he comes back out ages later, 'im to tell you the Rineys are leaving' he says and stands at the open door, 'and ive promised Mum youll both behave'

so we know hes not joking and we march down the

back stairs side by side *clump-clump clump-clump* and i want to kiss Di because she looks so *sulky*,

'goodbye goodbye goodbye' the Rineys call,

and we stamp across the street in step though we dont dare to poke out our tongues in case Michael catches us, and Mum leans into the car to kiss Miriam and then its Mikes turn,

'Aunty Mirrie' he says 'would you like to see Arthur?'

'and whos Arthur, dear?' she asks,

and while she gives him a big smile with her bright red lips my gut starts twisting up because i *know*!

Mike unbuttons his shirt,

and suddenly Aunt Mirrie flings her fat body back in the seat and her face goes purple and her huge mouth opens wide and she SCREAMS so loud that people walking on the other side of the street stop to stare, and Mike backs off,

'Dods!' Aunt Miriam shrieks,

because his pet snake is curled up all warm and snoozing against his chest,

'Dods!' Uncle Dick roars behind the wheel,

and Mike skips out of reach,

'the thought of that—' Aunt Miriam shudders in her fur coat 'that *slimy* creature hiding there all through lunch! you horrid boy!' she shrieks 'you horrid horrid boy! sitting next to me to eat! oh i feel sick! sick! sick!'

and the car shoots off like a rocket all black and glittering,

'poor Mirrie' Mum says and shes laughing so much there are tears in her eyes, but Mikes cross 'Arthurs a harmless grass snake' he says 'and he gets frightened by loud noises'

and while i wait in the butchers queue with Mum she teaches me to read the sign WHALE MEAT FOR SALE and there are chunks of it in the window because whale meat is dark red and locks disgusting and inside the shop theres sawdust on the floor and some of its got blood mixed up with it and i dont want to be in this queue,

'but queues are a good thing' Mum says 'queues are what make us civilised'

and this surprises me so that i look around at the people lined up behind us,

and we go to Miss Wilkinses Infants and Miss Wilkins makes us stand in line for drill but my gasmask gags me and the rubber farts against my cheeks, and after the bell i fetch a pencil and begin drawing so i can think about my first day at school that was *awful* because we were too early and the chairs were still upside down on the desks and i was left alone, and when the other kids came they poked their tongues out at me and i cried and looked for Di, though she was so furious she pushed me away,

'stop clinging to *me*' she said 'im in second class'

and we take turns standing on the step of the X-ray machine at the shoe shop where i put my feet in the slot at the bottom like im shown while Mr Higgins looks into the machine at the top,

'the best new shoes leave room for your feet to grow' he says,

and now im allowed to look for myself and this is fun because i stare into the glass screen down at my feet a long long way below me right at the bottom and they look like green bones in green jelly toes, and they look too far off to be mine though they *are* and i can prove it by wiggling them,

'one day' Mr Higgins says 'we shall have a machine so big we can see your whole skeleton'

and now Di has her go,

'angel feet' she says,

and what puzzles me about growing is why we cant ever catch ourselves doing it, even while Gran keeps saying what a *big* boy i am i still feel little, though this is my secret that she mustnt know because she says i have footballers knees too, and we wear our new shoes into the street and theyre completely waterproof! so you can stamp in puddles and its okay,

'the shoes are a present from Gran' Mum says,

i have to share the bath with Mike so we can save water and gas, but what i see is that his willie has an extra bit of skin and i dont like the look of it,

'what?' he says,

and i slosh around to get my wooden duck bobbing on the waves so i dont have to look,

but Mike laughs nastily,

does this mean theres something wrong with mine?

and we hang around the railway station watching old men up ladders taking down the towns name, and theres a conductor who always talks to us,

'so now' he says 'German commandos parachuting into the parish wont know where they are'

'will they be lost?' i ask him,

'lost and wandering i dont know where' he says 'so then they can be easy caught'

but one sign wont come off so it has to be bashed with a hammer,

and an army truck stops outside the goods yard so some troops jump out to line up in a row and they look grumpy but because theyre soldiers they have to keep their heads still while their eyes switch about,

can ~~*yuo*~~ *you see me from up in heven?*

BANG! and then the sound of bombers drones away to nothing and that one bang is all there is, but now i can hear a single plane rumbling in and its so loud its going to dive into the town because its too low to miss us, and im sick of being under the piano and im hot and Di has got the torch that she shines in my eyes while the noise gets louder and louder even though i stick my fingers in my ears and something must be wrong with it because the motors coughing,

'i reckon hes been hit' Mike says,

'will he crash on top of us?' i say,

‘no’ Mike says ‘but i dare say he wont get further than the common’

‘i hope he does crash’ i say ‘then we can go up and look at the wreck’

‘youll do no such thing, young man’ says Mum,

and the roar passes right over our roof so that you can feel it in the piano, but Dis busy looking at one of Mums photos and she hunches away from me so i cant see,

‘dont cheat’ she says,

‘cheat yourself!’ i tell her

and the bomber drones away and coughs and drones,

‘ssh, darlings’ says Mum,

‘its my *turn*!’ i say ‘bloody bloody—’

but Di holds the snapshot out of my reach even though we are all cramped up, so i give her my tiger growl, teeth and all,

‘Rodney Hall!’ Mum warns,

and i growl again for good luck and snatch the torch,

‘pass it on, Diana’ Mum says ‘there are plenty more to come’

so i snatch it off her,

‘who are these dummies?’ i ask,

‘thats a family picnic’ Mum tells me,

and i get a good close look,

‘but we dont know *them*’ i say,

‘we often had picnics like that, though the flies!’ Mum says ‘youd never imagine so many flies!’

and i can still hear that enemy bomber coughing and droning away alone, so maybe Michael was wrong and it wont crash,

'we used to ride horses all day and make camp at night' Mum says 'and sit around poking at the fire'

the sky outside goes quiet,

'do they have air raids in Kangaroo Valley?' i say,

'no darling' Mum says 'the war is only here'

i get busy picking at a scab on my knee and at last the all-clear starts up, and we can hear voices from the street below and a man in steel-capped boots running *clip clip, clip clip* the whole way down towards the railway station, so when Mum gets up we scramble out and make a dash for the window and out there the sun is just coming up,

'its tomorrow' Mike says,

and everythings still and quiet,

'well thats the first raid i ever heard of with only one bomb' Mum says 'anyway, we are safe'

and she kisses us all and goes into the kitchen while we stay at the window to watch, but she can guess,

'now now, you children!' she calls,

because here come the usual women and they stroll across the street to hang around the telephone booth,

'are those *tarts* there again?' Mum says and shes banging things on the stove already 'is that what youre watching?'

'no' i say,

but Diana and Michael have mesh marks printed on their noses,

'are they widows?' i ask because Mums a widow,

'dont be a dope' Mike says,

and the secret is that Mums husband died before the war, so his death doesnt mean anything and i cant remember him,

'one might as well live in Gomorrah!' Mum grumbles,

and i know Gomorrah is the word for an important place,

everything in the street is wet and empty,

'look!' says Mike,

and we can see for ourselves, across the road the funeral parlour is *gone* and i wish Mum was here to hold my hand,

and theres just a big hole and Roger Sawyer is looking down into it,

'hullo Roger' i call out,

Dis got her skipping rope so she starts skipping,

and Rogers fathers looking into the hole too, and hes our undertaker and theyre sipping hot cocoa because i can smell it even over here and Roger is friends with Mike,

so i call out 'where did you get the cocoa!'

and they wave and look cosy in scarves and gloves,

'hullo there' calls Mr Sawyer,

Di stops skipping and we cross over and Mr Sawyer shows us the hole and its *huge*,

'it makes you think' he says,

and i can see Rogers been crying because theres nothing left of their shop,

'lucky there was no one home, just three corpses' Mr Sawyer says,

and Mike starts laughing till hes laughing so much he doubles up and he staggers around like an idiot,

'whats so funny?' i ask,

and i hit him because he doesnt share the joke, but he grabs my head in a headlock and shoves me back towards home,

and i know lots of things and for instance i know water runs downhill and not the other way because thats what water *is*, and its fun here in the gutter making a dam and i let it dribble through a bit at a time and now i can put stones in the way and watch it sneak around them, and an empty cigarette packet comes floating down to get caught,

and Gran tells me the big picture in her room is an *oil painting* but i reckon its a few cows flopping in the shade under a knobbly tree,

and shes got an armchair you can stand on for a better look and shes got some little tables too and a huge carpet and windows with round tops and curtains down to the floor and outside theres a garden that the gardener comes to do,

so Gran complains about money all the time but when she wants us kids to run errands or when she wants us to give her kisses she bribes us with pennies and sometimes threepences and she gives the best hugs because of the way she catches hold of you to squeeze you against her and her cheeks are so soft and puffy i like kissing them and i can smell cooking smells and i touch her hair that she does in a bun, and if you pop in early enough you can catch her sitting at the dressing-table with her hair out loose and all long and white and she has a go at it with the brush, and every day she gives it a hundred strokes,

and Gran goes to church but we dont, and instead of a number her house has a name New Mills Court with a cellar underneath thats like dungeons and upstairs she keeps a *chamber pot* under her bed in among the fluff and feathers, because ive seen it and its made of thick china with tulips painted on and i know she uses it at night because she has to empty it in the morning and that must mean she squats down on it and Mum calls this Victorian,

'will you fetch me the newspaper?' Gran says,

'how much?' i say,

'all you think of, i suppose' says Gran 'is ice-cream'

'whats ice-cream?' i say,

and Joan lives with Gran because shes Mums sister but we never call her aunty because shes not much bigger than Michael and we just call her Joan but we love her because you can ask her things, but she shakes her head when i ask about Gomorrah, so theres something she wont tell,

we all have to share the new butterfly net that Joans given us, and at the end of a *whole* afternoon weve only caught two lousy fritillaries and a cabbage white and Mike wont go for the tortoiseshell on the nettles because one wings damaged and he says it isnt good enough,

'anyway butterflies are *boring*' i say,

and the dopey things weve already caught perch on the twigs we put in their jar,

'what we need' i tell him 'is a swallowtail'

‘you dont say!’ Mike scoffs,

‘Miss Wilkins taught us about butterflies’ says Di ‘and they only live for a single day’

and she takes the net off me because its her turn,

‘then a *butterfly minute*’ i say ‘must last for ages’

but Michael ticks me off like he always does,

‘a minute is never more than a minute and a day is never more than a day, Rod’ he says,

and suddenly out of nowhere theres a peacock butterfly fluttering and bobbing our way,

‘is it?’ i say,

‘yes, a real peacock’ Mike says and his eyes are shining,

and we watch it settle on a thistle flower, just like that, wings opening and shutting,

‘look at those colours!’ Mike whispers,

so its bad luck that Di is the one with the net,

‘give it back!’ i say,

but shes not listening to me and she goes red in the face and she brings the net swishing down,

‘oh well done!’ Mike shouts,

because she got it but i wanted to get it,

and on the way home past the gasworks we meet Joans friend Sybil so we show her our special butterfly, and Di wont shut up about how quick she was but *i* tell Sybil that i saw it first and Mike holds up the glass jar with the peacock in, and the best thing is that it cant fly away and its *ours* and i see its velvety wings and i love it, so Sybil walks some of the way home with us and i run on ahead and up the stairs two at a time because i want to be first to tell Mum,

'Di got—' i yell 'and Sybil said—'

'dont shout' Mum says and she holds her head,

so i go straight to the kitchen cupboard and get out her big glass bowl so we can start gassing our specimens, and Mike gets busy pouring some ammonia from the bottle into an eggcup and hes careful not to spill a drop because its dangerous stuff and we put the perforated zinc cover on the eggcup, and the upside-down glass bowl over that, and already i can smell the *evaporation* so the ammonia must be poisoning me,

Mum watches but she pulls a face,

so i tell her 'gassing is the kindest way, Mum'

'ready, Di' Mike says 'bring him over'

but somehow Diana has taken hold of the jar with both hands and she turns her back on us so we cant see, and shes got the peacock all to herself and she starts carrying him out into the yard,

'hey, Mike!' i say,

'what do you know!' he says,

and while we watch she walks away with her knees all wonky,

'Di!' Mike yells when she gets to the top of the stairs,

but she doesnt even look back and shes gone and

when we chase her shes right down the end of the lane and what we see is her snapping the rubber band from around the jar,

'whats shes *doing*?' i say,

because shes ripping the paper cover off,

but doesnt she realise theres nothing to stop the peacock escaping now?

'go!' she says to the butterfly and holds the jar up,

and she shakes the jar,

NO!

but the peacock seems to like it in there, so she shakes it again,

'help' i whisper,

and then he goes fluttering free, and i see the markings on his wings like big eyes, up above the elderberry tree and up above the old Shell oil shed,

'well' says Mike 'thats the end of all our hopes'

and he takes the empty jar from Di and he doesnt hit her, but i want to hit her, and he leads the way back upstairs, so the only thing to do is go indoors to tell Mum, but not me because i stay out in the yard leaning over the parapet and i spit down into the neighbours place and stare at peoples roofs and listen to the pips on the radio sets down there because its the BBC news, and its getting dark,

and some swallows flit through the air above my head so i can hear the snip of their beaks, hunting

but if you were here id like to ask you about Mikes idea when he says the world is spinning like a top, because i reckon things would fall off of Australia,

but here in England they blow up instead,

and this is our first time seeing a film at night but wouldnt you guess! right in the middle of everything the air raid sirens go off! damn damn! and the manager comes out on the stage in front of Tarzan whos still wrestling a crocodile and he tells us we have to make haste,

'ladies and gentlemen' he roars 'do not panic'

but everybody heads for the doors and the public shelter outside,

'do not panic!' people say and some of them laugh 'watch out' they say 'i can see you panicking there!'

and we move as quick as we can out into the street where the whole night sky is glowing, and Mum looks up at it,

'Bristols burning' she murmurs,

so i keep hold of Dis sleeve or we are going to get lost among the legs and shoes and Mum says something to me but its hard to hear in all this racket, and now someone pushes down on my head and when i look its an old man and hes only got one arm but he leans on me like a walking stick, 'watch out' he tells the crowd around us 'for the little chap down here under your feet'

and we shuffle forward waiting our turn,

'another blitz!' i tell Mike,

but Mike says 'no, *London* gets blitzed'

'so do we'

'no, this is just bombing'

'its a blitz!' i yell at him,

and here we go down underground so everythings going to be alright,

'don't you ever listen?' Mike says 'the blitz is much bigger'

but i know hes scared because he squeezes my hand,

so into the shelter we go and lots of people are here already,

now suddenly no ones holding my hand,

'Mum!' i shout,

and here she is and she picks me up to carry me the rest of the way,

'i don't like it here' i tell her,

'i know, darling' she says,

but we keep pushing in and the place is big and dim and Michael finds a bench for us to sit on up against the wall, but its uncomfortable and because of the awful stink i hold my nose,

'pooh!' says Di,

and that starts me giggling so Mum puts me down,

and people are sitting under rotten light bulbs in wire cages and they watch us while more people keep arriving down the steps, but at least weve got away from the din of those sirens,

THUD, the first bomb happens,

and Mum takes off one of her gloves so she can comb my hair with her fingers,

and women with scarves tied round their heads get busy opening paper twists of boiled lollies to share around, and bent old men turn a wooden crate upside down and crouch around it and deal out some playing cards with knobbled fingers, and theres even a family loaded with blankets making beds down here,

'lucky them' i say because its cold,

'poor darling' says Mum 'we were caught too far from home to fetch warm things'

'im cold'

'so am i' Di says,

'sos everybody' says Mike,

and theres Mrs Arbuthnot who smiles hullo and takes some knitting out of her bag and gets busy clicking away like mad and i swing my legs because my feet dont touch the floor and the lady next to Mum lights up a cigarette and gives one to Mum and they talk in quiet voices and puff away together, and i wish i had a cigarette too,

THUD THUD,

the explosions are so close the bench shivers and

i can feel the shivers through my bottom, and now a whole lot of children rush down the steps and come clattering in, but they stop once theyre in the door so that the ones coming behind have to crowd up against them, and theyve got runny noses and theres this bossy woman who lines them up and she hunts around to find room for them to sit, but they still crowd together like idiots and ready for trouble too and they stick their hands in their pockets and sniffle, and she rolls her eyes at me when she sees me watching, but im not going to side with *her*,

'are they orphans?' i whisper to Mike,

'i expect so' Mike whispers back 'evacuees'

WHOMP!

a crack zigzags down the wall from the ceiling to the floor and people point it out,

'we shall be alright, see?' says Mum 'the walls holding up'

but two little orphans start wailing and theyre girls and theyre smaller than me, and each ones got a label pinned on her jacket so maybe theyve been bombed out already and they wail and sob,

'ssh, you two' says the old bat 'i shall be with you when i can'

but Mum drops her cigarette on the floor and unfolds her handkerchief and she goes across to wipe their tears and she wipes their noses too and she tells them to blow, and afterwards she drops the handkerchief on the ground and leaves it there, but she lifts one child on each arm and brings them back to us, and their shoes make smudges on her skirt and i try to point this out while they settle their heads against her shoulders and bury their grubby faces in her fur collar, just where *i* want to be, and they turn their eyes up to look at her.

6

But this is our first parcel ever and it comes by post and its wrapped in cloth and sewn up with stitches and the label has lots and lots of stamps stuck all over it,

'i bags the pink kangaroos' i say,

because theres a whole block of them,

'you cant' Diana says 'theyve got to be shared out'

'sez who?' i say,

'stamps are worth more in a block' Mike explains to her 'and thats a fact'

and 'i saw them first, so theyre mine' i say 'anyway i dont have any kangaroos in my album'

Di yells at me 'its not fair!'

and i give her my tiger growl,

'shut up, you two' Mike says 'or i shall take the whole lot for myself right now'

and he *would*,

'anyway' he says 'whats inside may be even better than the stamps'

'what do you think it is, Mike?' i ask,

'havent the foggiest'

'toys?' says Di,

he picks it up and thinks,

'its too heavy for toys' he says,

'well' i say 'weve got to keep it safe till Mum gets home from work'

so i weigh the parcel in my hands and i can feel a good strong box under the cloth but nothing rattles even when i shake it and nothing shifts about even when i tip it upside down,

and Mike takes it off me and he places it right in the middle of the table,

and we get on with the household chores but we stay close to it, so Di sweeps the lino around the table and i do the drying up with my back to the sink and Michael washes the dishes while he keeps looking over his shoulder,

and at long last we hear the latch click down at the bottom of the outside stairs, so Mums home and Di and i run across the yard to hurry her up, and at last she climbs to the top and we tell her,

'this must be a food parcel from Australia' Mum says,

and the headache begins to clear from her face and she gets busy with scissors to cut the stitching and takes the cloth wrap off and opens the cardboard box inside,

'you must shut your eyes' Mum says 'and take a lucky dip'

so we all reach in,

and Di fishes out a pot of jam,

'melon and lemon' Mum says,

and this sounds really peculiar and then Mike gets a tin of pineapple, whatever thats like,

but i only get tinned butter, so i lose,

'butter is best of all' Mum says and she gives me a squeeze 'youre always the lucky one!' and then she starts setting all the rest of the stuff out on the table and we get a good look at strange labels on tins of corned beef and weird stuff called asparagus and peanut butter and other things, and theres a note inside the parcel written by a typewriter that says *sent with love and best wishes from Winifred*,

'is the fire lit in the lounge?' says Mum,

'yes' i say and im hopping up and down,

so we all troop in there with our toasting forks and some crumpets to try out the butter and the jam,

but i still dont understand who Winifred is,

ive stolen Mikes bunch of keys and theyre in my pocket and they feel huge and heavy banging against my leg when i run and Mikes going to *brain* me when he finds out, because keys are important,

and we are out picking wild flowers when Di finds some cowslips and theyre her favourites and she offers one to Mum so she can smell it,

'one day' Mum says to her 'youll remember this'

and Di holds Mums hand,

next thing some *man* arrives wearing civvies and wheeling his brand new Raleigh bicycle across our yard,

'hes a detective' Mum explains 'hes coming to stay'

'why?' i ask 'is he an evacuee?'

'no, but he has been billeted on us'

and we all know what billeted means because its what happens to those orphans when families have to take them in and feed them and have to give them somewhere to sleep, and i watch him wheeling his bike right up to our door and he knocks though he can see us through the glass,

'come in' says Mum and she gives him a cup of tea straight off,

'thank you' he says,

and he takes it and drinks standing up holding the saucer in one hand and the cup in the other, and his trenchcoats damp on the shoulders and the belt is tight round his waist and hes so huge the kitchen is full of cold air, 'my name is Guy' he tells us all,

'why dont you have a label on?' i ask him,

'grown-ups dont need labels' says Mum,

'not even if theyre evacuees?' i ask,

but Mum just leads the way into the lounge room,

'youll sleep here, Guy' she says and shows him our settee,

so he tries it out on the spot and when he lies down his feet hang out a long way off the end but he looks pleased and he doesnt seem to realise that this is half of our safety tunnel when theres an air raid and there will be no room for him in there with us under the piano keys because we are already too crowded,

but Guy finds the right corner for putting his leather bag and he has come to stay, so i show him the gas meter,

'it only takes shillings in the slot' i explain 'and you have to turn this knob till you hear the coin fall down inside'

and he pops a couple in,

'its too soon' i tell him because he hasnt used any gas yet,

and Guy ruffles my hair but Michael gives me a furious look,

'it will be a comfort to have a man around the house' Mum says,

and straight away he gets to work fixing the bent gas tap on the stove, the very job weve struggled with ever since it happened when Diana and i dropped that pot full of cold water we were lifting and made a terrible mess that took a lot of mopping up,

Guy is setting off to work so he hoists his new bike on one shoulder to carry it down the stairwell and weve come out to lean over the parapet and watch him down there wheeling it away along the lane,

'where does he go?' Di says,

'what does he do?' i say,

'he must be part of the war effort' Mike says,

'but what does he *do*?'

'well' says Mike 'detectives solve crimes'

'what crimes?' i say,

'any crimes' says Mike,

'but why does he solve his crimes *here*?' i say,

'you are going to drive me up the wall!' Mike groans,

so it must be a puzzle and puzzles are what i like best in all the world,

pissing is a naughty word but not the worst one i know,

‘cuckoos are special’ Mike explains ‘because they push their brothers and sisters out of the nest’ and he gives us a good hard look,

but we squat in this field and we are too busy picking mushrooms, and thats definitely a cuckoo we can hear calling,

‘its the first sign of spring’ says Mum straightening up and pushing her hands against her back,

and somewhere way away in the woods the cuckoo calls *cuck-oo* again,

and Mums home early but she ticks us off,

‘i wont have you children being rude to Guy’ she says,

‘but hes always here!’ Mike says ‘he never leaves us in peace!’

‘Mr Churchill gives us no choice’ she says,

and we know its Mr Churchill who gave her her job,

‘hes always listening and looking’ says Di,

‘well, hes detecting’ Mike explains,

so that gives me a creepy feeling because perhaps he can detect when im afraid of him,

‘it could be a lot worse’ Mum says,

though she doesnt explain how,

and in he comes just when weve begun to laze around and stare into the fire, 'righto, kids' he says 'out in the yard for some cricket practice'

and i like playing catch, though Mike pretends he doesnt,

'have you ever been a soldier, Guy?' i ask him,

he shakes his head,

'soldiers are lucky' Guy tells me with a wink 'because they escape their families'

and i dont understand, but theres a wind getting up and i feel a bit of a shiver,

so im glad to stay the night with Gran, but now Gran says i have to share the *bed* with Great-Uncle Mont! and Great-Uncle Mont is terrifically old but he listens when i tell him things, though i dont want him in my bed so i hang around with Gran in her room,

'have you said your prayers?' she says,

and she has a Jesus on the wall made out of bone and it hangs from a hook and Jesus is all muscles but his head hangs down and hes got little spikes through his hands and a spike through his feet, and Gran shows me how to kneel beside the bed,

'can i say the prayers in my head?' i ask,

and she says 'thats the best way'

and Gran shows me how to put my hands together,

so i ask Jesus for a bike and a cream bun and for Great-Uncle Mont to go and sleep at his own house,

'off you go now' says Gran 'thats a good boy'

so theres no way out and i trudge into the bedroom,

and Great-Uncle Mont is standing in his shoes and *coms*! and i have to cough to stop myself laughing because coms are so hilarious, but whats awful is his shakes that he got when he was in the army in the other war, and i know already that shakes like this are called shell-shock, and they get his head going all by itself and he has a deep shuddery voice,

'c-o-m-m-e along in-n-n' he says,

and he tries to light his pipe but this is difficult because his lips are shaking, so the pipe bobs up and down and even when his big shaky hands manage to strike the match theres a problem getting them to meet, because the flame goes one way and the pipe goes the other, and some spit dribbles out from the corner of his mouth while hes busy sucking the stem and missing,

but now he gets it, so the tobacco glows and he puffs out a big cloud of smoke and he rumbles because hes happy, and already the bedrooms full of smoke and i don't know why but i love the smell of it, and he turns away while i undress and get into my pyjamas and i check to see hes not looking and i can see his bald patch and his huge hairy ear,

'goodnight, son' Great-Uncle Mont says,

but now he takes his pipe out because hes going to lie down in bed and his old hand goes groping for the bedside lamp so he can turn off the switch, but his knuckles knock against it and i reckon we are going to be *electrocuted*, but he brings it off and now we are in the dark,

'goodnight' i whisper,

and i lie straight as i can right on the edge of the bed and try not to think of anything, but thats impossible because he starts snoring and i cant help listening and i cant go to sleep so i just lie here thinking about ghosts and i reckon i can hear things in this bedroom even although i cant *see* anything spooky on my side of the room,

and im uncomfortable because at any moment i might fall out on the floor, wishing it *was* a ghost in the room with me, then at least i could have the bed to myself and i remember Grans stories about ladies in castles walking down the staircase to get revenge for something that was done before they died and i get scared now my eyes are used to the dark,

'Uncle Mont' i whisper,

and i give the old man a dig in the back with my elbow because a ghost would be worse than anything and Great-Uncle Mont lets out the biggest shakiest snore of all so i have to stick my fingers in my ears,

i ask Guy about ghosts, but he lifts me up off the floor and holds me so my eyes are level with his,

'theres no such thing in the world as ghosts' Guy says 'understood?'

and he gives me a bit of a shake, but Gran believes she has got one in her house, so i reckon that shed know,

'understood?'

when i dip my hands in the canal is warm, and green, and we get set up for a spot of tadpole fishing, so i fill the jars with water and put them in a line along the path that Mike says is called a bridle path, and i wipe my hands on my pants and im happy here and we are ready to begin, so next its up to Mike because hes got a good grip on the pole that belongs with his wigwam and hes delving right down in the mud to hoist up a big clump of weed that he dumps on the bank,

now we get busy with our fingers and this is the mucky part,

and Mike goes for another and sure enough theres tadpoles struggling here and we find our first-ever newt,

and Mike says 'no one really believes those stories about a giant pike living at the bottom of this canal'

and ive got my fingers in among the weed and im feeling about in there but i look down into the green water and i think something big *is* shifting along in secret, and i start to worry and my hair prickles when i see some sludgy ripples,

'oy!' i shout because this fish must be bigger than me and maybe half as long as the whole canal, and i rescue our jars with the tadpoles swimming about in them, so we all run away to flop on the soft grass where its safe to watch,

but nothing happens,

theres just bees humming and i can smell wild parsley,

'what can a pike do to you?' Di asks,

'a six-foot pike' Mike says 'oooh!'

'can it bite your leg off?' Di asks,

'probably' Mike says 'just like an angry swan can break your arm flapping its wing'

but i say 'where are the *swans*?'

for goodness sake!

'everythings too quiet' Di says,

and the water is still and green with a dragonfly stuck on its reflection,

'even so the world is turning under us' Mike says,

and i think this is ridiculous because youve only got to look to see that it isnt,

and its playtime, but before she lets us out Miss Wilkins claps her hands,

'children' she says 'you need to be brave'

and bits of her grey hair come loose from her bun,

'its the war' she says 'the war gets worse and worse'

but i dont know what that means,

'and England is doing its best'

and we sit behind our desks looking at her because we cant guess whats coming next or whether we are supposed to repeat after her,

'it doesnt bear thinking about' Miss Wilkins says 'but we could lose, and thats the dreadful truth'

so playtime is totally spoilt because nobody feels like racing around or laughing at all because every-ones been to the Gaumont and seen the Movietone news from the frontline, so we stand round with our friends and shrug our shoulders and stick our hands in our pockets, and the boys whove got coins jingle them,

my collars up and i have to walk backwards against the rain and against the wind too, and the back of my knees is getting wet and theres water in my shoes, but i dont care because im in second class and that means im growing up and ever since my birthday i dream about stealing a bike to try it out, and although Guys bike is too big to get my leg over thats my idea,

i *want*
to go fast
~~love~~

because im alone i can wander about for as long as i like and everybody knows this bookshop is called WH Smiths because there are books on all the shelves and childrens books on the tables, and i find an Enid Blyton and i get a good idea,

so, is anybody watching me?

no,

i pop it under my jersey just like that,

and i cant breathe in case something dreadful happens now,

but when i look up, all there is is quiet people turning the pages or poking around in their purses, so i stare at an atlas thats open but i dont really see anything,

i reach for the door and im out into the street,

i scram because otherwise someones going to catch me, i have to dodge among the ladies with their shopping baskets, and my arms are pistons, speeding away down the hill towards Gloucester Road to duck round the corner and hide behind Tucks bakers shop where i get in among the rubbish bins, and i take a pencil out of my pocket and write my name inside the front cover,

there!

because the good thing about writing your name in a book is that this is how you make it yours, and if any grown-ups stop me now and ask what im doing with it they can see for themselves, so i peep out in case i can spot someone chasing me and then i begin to walk home the long way through the park where its safer than the street, and im a real robber and everybody knows me so i have to keep moving, but what worries me is the problem of where to hide this book because theres no hope of keeping anything secret from Michael in our bedroom, and theres nowhere else in the flat that Di wont notice, and worst of all if *Guy* comes to know hes sure to call the police and i shall get put in prison and theyll make Mum pay a fine to let me out,

and the more i think about it the worse it is, and the only thing to do is put it back where i got it from,

back in the main street again i keep walking past the window outside WH Smiths, pretending to look through the glass at the books and i hope no one in theres watching me, but i dont know how to go in because i dont dare, and so i dither like Mike says i do when hes mad at me and this is awful, ‘hullo Rod’ says Roger Sawyer,

and i just grab the door handle and now i have to go through with it, so i step inside under the jingling bell and my ears are burning because Mrs Arbuthnot looks up to see, but i go straight to the table where theres the pile of Enid Blyton books and im praying to Jesus to stop my ears burning because theyre going to give me away! and i pick up one book and then another with the same story in it, and this is like charades because i have to pretend, and i pretend i cant decide, but the shop ladies are too busy dinging the till and wrapping up books to take a scrap of notice and theres plenty of time, so i slip the stolen one out from under my jersey,

all done!

Mrs Arbuthnot calls out ‘are you looking for something, Rodney?’

‘n-no, thank you’

and i can feel my face is redder than ever so i make a getaway,

‘goodbye dear’ she calls,

im back at the door and she waves from behind the counter, but im out!

and i wish you were here so you could give Mike a thrashing because even big boys cry if theyre hit hard enough,

now Mike says im big enough to play truant with him but hes playing truant from the big school and im only a truant from Miss Wilkinses Infants, though im happy its just us together doing something wrong, and we take our sandwiches down to the canal,

'youll be okay' he tells me 'because the whole town is up in arms against Miss Wilkins anyway'

and i can see them up in arms and all with guns and swords,

'why?'

'because of what she told you kids about losing the war' he tells me 'and the Home Guard wants to shut her school down'

'Mum says if it was in Kangaroo Valley it would be okay' i say,

'i told you before that youre an idiot' Mike says 'because you dont know the first thing about Australia'

'i do, i know'

'its way down at the bottom of the world'

'why?'

'what kind of question is why?'

'my kind of question'

'just get this into your head' he says 'to go to Sydney you have to sail across the Atlantic Ocean and then the Mediterranean Sea and then the Indian Ocean and *then* the Pacific'

'why are some called oceans and some called seas?'

'ask Miss Wilkins' he says 'one day when youre not playing truant'

and we dodge under the bridge because theres someone coming,

'i will' i promise,

'anyway if id thought you were going to talk the whole time' Mike says 'i wouldnt have let you come'

we three walk along the edge of the railway track to get a closer look because theres a train stopped on the siding with steam up,

'he cant chase us off' Mike says 'he has to stay in his engine'

'lets dare him!' i say,

and Di says 'its only a boring old freight train'

'shunting'

'pick up a couple of stones' Mike tells us 'in case he chases us and we need to chuck them at him'

and we are all good chuckers and good runners too,

but the driver takes no notice and keeps on wiping the brass handrails,

'get ready to run' Di whispers,

but instead i dart right up to the engine,

'hullo mister' i say,

and the driver leans out to look down and a cloud of steam gets me coughing,

'wanna climb up here for a bit of a look around?' he says,

'truly?'

'suit yourself' he says,

but Mike pushes past me so he can be first and then Di pushes past and im left behind and the steps are very steep and high off the ground, but once we are up there the driver gives me first turn trying out his seat and im allowed to take hold of the steel levers,

'theyre so smooth and warm' i say,

'can i try?' says Di,

'course you can, darlin' says the driver 'just dont start us going'

'shall we fetch some lumps of coal for you?' i ask 'for the fire?'

and thats why im standing getting too hot because the furnace door is open and i know there has to be a good blaze to heat the boiler,

'take the shovel with you' the driver says,

but the shovel is too big to manage even for Michael

so we cross over the bridge into the tender and bring back some lumps in our hands to throw into the furnace,

'thats the ticket' the driver says 'those should get me another mile closer to London'

and just up ahead the signal clunks from Stop to Go,

'times up' he tells us,

'thank you, driver' Diana says,

and Michael shakes his hand and then we all jump down and i get out my train-spotting book to find the number and i draw a huge star beside it, and now hes going i forgot to say goodbye,

under the station clock we fool around pretending weve got platform tickets and dodging into the toilets to escape the porters and then we head for the waiting-rooms,

'steam locomotion' Mike explains 'is a scientific marvel'

i run my finger across the timetable pasted on the wall and i can recite the station names that i know by heart and Mike offers to help some passengers sitting there,

'if you want to choose the best connections' he says 'we can tell you'

'thank you all the same' says a lady sounding high and mighty 'we shall catch the four forty' 'but that train always runs late' Mike warns her,

'nevertheless—'

'and it stops at every station' he says 'so youre better to wait for the four fifty-two direct'

'it might be worth our while to check' says another lady,

'my brother knows everything' i tell them 'and its because the last stationmaster used to give us tea'

'in pannikins' Di adds,

'and he told us hed offer us jobs' i remember,

'if it wasnt for the Union' Mike says,

'but he died' i tell them in case they get the wrong idea,

'or left' Di says,

'and now the *signalman* hates us' i say,

'and he chases us' Di says,

'so thats why we keep going back there' i tell the ladies 'just to get him mad'

out on the tracks we squat down between the lines to put our pennies on the rails so theyll be flattened out and i get a bright idea,

'weve got so much money it might be enough to *go* somewhere'

'children have to have a grown-up with them' Di says,

'but wholl know?' i say,

and because Gran gave Mike sixpence for mending her spectacles and because we have another fourpence between us and because thats enough to buy three half-singles third-class to Stonehouse with a penny left over we decide to go,

'but wheres Stonehouse?' i ask when the train comes,

and Mike says 'a couple of miles'

a couple of *miles*!

and we are in and it smells lovely and sooty but while we argue about which compartment we are going to sit in a soldier pushes past and bangs the door shut so we choose the corridor instead and stand leaning there with our elbows on the sill and sticking our heads out to watch the train roll away from the station and gather speed, and the telegraph poles go batting away behind us,

'if we measured the distance between the poles' Mike says 'we could calculate how fast we are going'

but i can *see* how fast we are going and i hang out as far as i dare so the wind can bang my hair about, and when weve had enough of that we set out along the swaying corridor to reach the end of the carriage, but between this carriage and the next i can see the ground skimming,

'dont be scared' says Mike 'just step straight over'

and this one is the first-class carriage so we give the seats a test and i let a window down on its leather strap and lean out again, but a scrap of soot flies into my eye though Mike says its okay and he makes me sit on the seat and uses his fingers to pull my face around,

'ive brought a hanky' Di says,

so she pokes at my eye to get the soot out. but the door slides open with a bang and an inspector in a cap clicks his punch at us while Mike shows our tickets,

'we spent all our pocket money on those' i tell him,

and Di pipes up 'are you going to put us in prison?'

so i could kill her,

but the inspector squints at her and he says 'no, lassie, you just pay a fine and that will do'

'but we cant' i say,

and Michael shows him our last penny,

'name?' the inspector says and he opens his notebook and takes out an indelible pencil to lick it with his horrid purple tongue while he gets ready to write,

'Roger Sawyer' Mike tells him,

and i cant believe my ears because hes the one who always tells us never to tell lies,

'what?' i yell and 'ow!' i yell,

because Mike kicks me,

'this is my sister' he says 'and thats my brother'

so the inspector writes down Roger Sawyer and Mike gives him Rogers address though i wiggle my eyebrows to remind him that Rogers house is *gone*,

'youll be hearing from us' says the inspector and then he shuts his book 'now, out with you!'

and he shoos us into the next car where the soldier looks up at us and glares so we sit on the edge of the hard seat and we dont dare speak while he can listen, but i get a good look at his rifle while ive got the chance,

'look at that' Di says and points because Stonehouse station still has the name up,

'it must be too small to matter' Mike explains,

and the soldier stands up suddenly and slings the rifle over his shoulder and he jumps to the ground on his hobnails, then we jump down too, and the locomotive chuffs steam and the wheels squeal and the couplings clatter,

'good riddance to bad rubbish!' i yell at the guards van when it passes,

but the soldier stops and looks back at me, so i point at the train to show him what i mean but im ready to run just the same,

'idiot!' Mike snarls at me under his breath,

but its alright though because the soldier pushes through the turnstile and hes out, and we can see some army tents in a field and a hut with smoke coming from the chimney pipe.

'what are we going to do?' Di wails,

'lets check the timetable' i say,

'so we can catch another train and get caught again?' Mike says 'and this time without any tickets at all?'

so we walk and the only way i can keep on walking is to get giddy watching the road pass under my feet but not as fast as the ground under the train, and we walk past hedges and we walk past fields till we are all tired and it starts to get dark,

'i cant go any faster' i say,

'stop grizzling' Mike says 'this is a Forced March and winning the war depends on us, because weve got the secret code so we have to keep in step like a proper army'

no one dares to say anything about Mum getting worried,

and i tap my boiled egg with a spoon the proper way to crack the shell, but Guy just takes hold of a knife and slices the top off his,

the boys in the gang roll up their sleeves like soldiers because that way they look tough and we watch them and they watch us, till Di and i step back out of sight under the roof of the railway station because Mike didnt come today so we dont have him to protect us, and anyway we know who these kids are because they sometimes try catching us on our way home from school, but they dont know that we can report them now weve got a *detective* at our place! so im all ready to run across the street and escape or at least give it a try when the hotel door bangs open and some drunks come out in a crowd, and drunks are the worst of all because theyre troops on leave from the war and one of them opens his buttons to do his business in the alley at the side of Harrises and i watch, and the kids in the gang start talking to the men and i wonder how they know them and what theyre saying and one day im going to join a gang,

and in Grans bathroom i get a good look at Great-Uncle Monts shaving brush and safety razor and his shaving soap and when he sits with me for breakfast Gran gives us toast and margarine with homemade marmalade,

'youll have to make do' she says 'we shant have butter till the end of the war' and Great-Uncle Mont shakes his head and his jaw is working at the toast so he has to slurp some tea to help it down and he reaches over to pat my knee,

'give my love to Dods' he says 'i have a soft spot for Dods'

'his mother' Gran tells him and she always nods her head to back up what she says 'is still true to Dick, God rest his soul'

and i know that everyone called Mums husband Dick even though he was christened Percy Edgar, 'poor Dick' says Great-Uncle Mont.

'hes sadly missed' says Gran,

but not by me! because i never even knew him, but i *do* remember an airman with POLAND on his shoulder speaking to Mum in Lewises shop, and afterwards she said she wouldnt put up with it, but i didnt take too much notice because theres a lot of things like that, and she even turns her nose up at us getting milk at school because it stands in crates getting warm on the school step, and she wrinkles her nose at the fish shop and she wont put up with boys on rollerskates,

Great-Uncle Mont uses both hands to steady his teacup and he watches me over the rim as if he can see what im thinking,

'the boy is a Hall through and through' he says 'he takes after his late uncle Ted'

'true enough' says Gran 'hes not a Buckland like Fred, thats for certain, nor a Gabb like you and me'

and this gets my goat, because i hate being talked about as if im not there and i can feel my ears burning, so i get down from the table and run upstairs to the bathroom and stand in front of the mirror looking in my face to find me, so i frown and i grin and im serious, but its just the same phizzog as always,

'we mustnt be late' Gran calls up to warn me,

so now its time to head off home and Guy will have

gone to work, so i jump downstairs three at a time and Grans carpets so thick i hardly make a sound,

'goodness gracious you *do* remind me!' she says,

and i race straight out through the open door,

'im nearly seven!' i shout back at her,

'youll have to wait for me because you cant walk home alone' she calls out after me and shes trying to stick a big hatpin into her hat 'im coming with you'

and in my dream i did swallow a pip and the tree grew and i couldnt get it out of me, but some girl in my dream promised that if i could only swallow her too she could get in there and cut it down for me,

things look the same as always because the street is the same and the rain is the same and the grocer is the same too, and hes getting the same stuff as usual down off the shelves and his moustache is all grey and hes got the same pencil stuck behind his ear and the same shelves behind him with a shelf of biscuits and a shelf of tomato sauce and a shelf of jam and a shelf of starch packets and a shelf of condensed milk, and im so tall now i can put my chin on the counter to watch what he does so i make sure he doesnt cheat us when he weighs out our sugar,

'youve only got enough coupons for half a pound' the grocer says,

'we know' says Di,

and the name on the scales is *Avery*,

and i can spell because im a school boy,

'A very' i explain to Mike in a whisper in case he hasnt seen,

and the grocer scoops some more from the sugar sack and i watch the needle creep up bit by bit, but the grocer gives me a dirty look while he folds the top of the bag and i give him a dirty look back,

'i wont be taking cheek from you, young fella-me-lad!' he says and reaches for a tin of golden syrup,

'what did he do this time?' Mike asks him,

and then he gets his hands round my neck to show the grocer how he could strangle me, but i love this syrup tin with its picture of bees flying round a sleeping lion because its all real gold and shiny green, and i watch the grocers scissors *snip* some coupons out of our ration books,

'whats next?' the grocer says and strokes his moustache and picks up our list,

'biscuits' says Mike,

'these?'

and the grocer sticks the pencil back behind his ear and licks his fingers to open a new paper bag that he fills with broken biscuits from a box because the broken ones are the cheapest,

and every day Diana and ive got to watch out that Mike doesnt get away and leave us behind, so when he goes out we chase him and catch up,

but this rooster in the fairytale has been cut in half so hes got only one wing and one leg and one eye and half a body, and everywhere he walks he has to hop, so no wonder hes bad-tempered and he wont stop to help anybody on his way to Madrid to see the King, but the Kings cook pops him in the dinner pot and though the half-rooster asks the cook to spare him he wont, and though he asks the water to spare him it wont, and nor will the fire and even the wind says no, and so the story finishes *and thats why he ends up on a church steeple turning this way and that way* and i remember every word,

but i still dont get it,

Mike starts chucking stones in the stream but its no good trying to skip them because he says you need a low bank to get the right angle, so instead of flat stones he bombs the stream with big chunky ones that crash into the wet pebbles and Di does the same, and so i choose a monster and i have to hitch my scarf out of the way before i can waddle over to the bank with it,

'crikey!' says Mike,

'this ones the biggest of all' i tell them,

and i go to heave it into the stream, but my cap flies off and im a goner YOUCH! and im swamped! and cold water pours down my collar and sleeves and up my pants and my knees hurt and my fingers hurt and i cant breathe, but i stagger up and my feet stumble on the slippery pebbles, and my chest wont let me breathe, and the stream rushes round my knees, and the screams i can hear are coming from the bank above, and i dont know if im crying or not because my face is streaming wet and my hair drips and im shivering all over and the best i can do is to wade to the edge,

'you forgot to let go of the stone' Di laughs 'that was the funniest thing in the world!'

but Mike takes hold of my elbow and hes already rescued my cap and he helps me up,

'one of those cottages' he says looking ahead down the stream 'has smoke coming from the chimney'

and my teeth chatter and somehow im laughing and

crying at the same time, but what i really feel is miserable and stupid and my knees hurt,

but the cottage lady says we are welcome and she muffles me up in a blanket and my wet clothes hang steaming on a clothesline above the stove and the whole kitchen is smoky and dark and there are flames in the cracks, and now she pulls a prickly vest over my head and then a shirt and a jumper with the elbows out,

'tell your mother this is all i can find for the present because my boys is wearing the good ones' she says 'i dont want her thinking'

and she tweaks my ear and i like her,

'most likely you youngsters already know my twins' she says,

and now that she laughs i can see shes got four teeth left and theyre all at the front,

but i dont want to tell her that her twins are in the gang that chases us after school,

and Mum throws up her hands,

'thats twice the washing i shall have to do now!' she says,

and she chucks the borrowed stuff in the washtub,

'i do wish youd be more responsible' she says and holds her head,

'*i* can wash them' i say,

'you can do nothing of the sort' she says,

because washing clothes is one job Mum always does and we never do,

'i suppose theres really no way out of paying her a visit to thank her' Mum says with a sigh 'will i never have a moment to myself!'

and our kettle is a dark blue that Mum calls royal blue but the dings in it show the metal underneath and its got a lid that can burn your fingers if you are not quick, and i bring Mum a cup of tea in bed and she blesses me even though shes in despair and she drinks it straight down without any sugar, ugh! and then she turns over and pulls the eiderdown up to her chin,

'whats that pencil doing behind your ear?' she says,

'im a grocer' i tell her,

and we three have our tea in the kitchen where weve started work on a cut-out castle,

'be careful to fold along the dotted lines' Mike says 'and glue them together'

'more tea, Mum?' i ask,

'no thank you, darling' says her muffled voice under the eiderdown, 'have you got rid of that pencil?'

our water pipes freeze and my ears hurt because the cold pinches them even though im wearing a balaclava and my is nose is running too and we are crossing the park on our way home from school and frosty dead leaves crunch under our shoes while we scuff along, and Dianas the luckiest because she finds a frozen cobweb and she breaks it off and she holds it out for me to see, and the cobweb is flat on her woollen hand,

'you mustnt touch it or youll snap it in two' she says,

and i say 'snap snap snap' to practise whistling the *s*es like Miss Wilkins,

and Di laughs till shes sick because we are thinking up all the words that ever had an *s* in them, and when Mum gets home i tell her,

'she makes a silver sound when she speaks'

and Mum laughs,

'as long as she teaches you manners'

'we have to fold our arms on the desk' i say 'to have a *sl*eep or at least a *sn*ooze'

Guy says he needs meat more than once a week and hes got the coupons,

i put the bookmark in page 87 so i can always find the picture where Gulliver is flat on his back and he cant move because the tiny beetle-size people swarming everywhere tie him down with a hundred threads,

Mike makes a collection tin for us by punching a slot in the top of a condensed milk can and sharing out the condensed milk inside because its our favourite, and afterwards he pours boiling water in to clean the stickiness out and then he gets to work with his fountain pen and prints a perfect label *For the Childrens Christmas*,

'do a Red Cross tin instead' i suggest,

but he wont and so we test the new tin like that because we are allowed to stay out after dark as long as we keep singing, and all through O Come All Ye Faithful our hopes are up because we sing so loud that a whole family of ladies come to listen at the open doorway,

'sweet' says the big one when we finish,

and a girl of fifteen or so gets given a half-crown to bring down to us,

and i hold out our new tin, keeping an eye on the coin while she bites her lip and its a glorious silver coin, because a half-crown must be the world record for carol singers, but she peers through her goggles at the slot, i shoot Michael a look,

and she even takes the tin out of my hand to rattle it because theres three pennies and the sixpence already in there, and she gets a good look at the label,

'its not for anybody' she calls over her shoulder,

'well just thank the children nicely, dear' her mother tells her 'and come inside'

the proper way to wear a scarf is to wind it round your neck then throw the end over your shoulder,

Mikes got us a sledge on loan and we can have it all day and the snow is thick at the golf links and all sparkling on the trees and there are other kids with their sledges but we find a quiet spot to ourselves,

'theres a knack to sledging' Mike says 'and i shall teach you'

'but we know already' i say 'you just sit on it and go'

'thats unless you want to stop' he says,

and because he has to have the last word he *lies* down on the sledge to show us,

'it hasnt got a brake so this way you can use your hands' he says, and next thing hes tricked us, already sliding away and im left standing at the top of the slope with Di watching him glide right down to the bottom,

'me next!' we both yell at the same time,

and we bang the snow off our gloves and wave our arms around while we watch him drag our sledge back up, and his face is all pink,

'this particular model has no steering either' he explains to Di 'its just metal runners nailed on to wood, alright? so you have to get a good grip and then lean to one side when you want to guide it'

so Di sits on, clutching the sides like shes told, she looks proud as all get out and the sledge sets off and bounces her around while she zooms away and when she gets off she waves and jumps up and down and her voice sounds tiny like a bird voice,

'one … where … must'

so im lucky last,

and now i know boys have to lie down and girls have to sit up, so Mike holds it steady while i lie face down on the wooden slats and get ready and the sledge feels big and suddenly the ground is too close,

'sure youre alright?' Mike says,

too late!

the sledge starts to move all by itself!

WOW! and theres nothing to do except hang on, HELP! and the snow swoops, WHOOPEE! with me clinging on like mad, and im scared to death and its the fastest thing ever,

everyone we know is on the lookout for butterfly bombs but no one ever seems to find any though we hunt under trees and bushes and we know they look like baked bean tins because we see the posters all around town and when they fall theres a hinge so the case opens out like a ladybirds wings, and they only go off when someone picks them up, so if we find one we mustnt touch it but we have to run and fetch the Home Guard instead,

and our paraffin oil heater makes the whole kitchen pong but Mums promised us a caraway seed cake so im waiting to lick the wooden spoon and the bowl as well, but Guy comes bursting out of the bathroom with a towel wrapped round his middle and we can hear the bathwater gurgle away and the drain sucking,

so its not true that all men have hairy chests,

and Mum frowns at him and whips the cake mixture, but he whistles and leaves wet footmarks on the lino in the corridor and shuts the lounge room door behind him and hes dresssed when he comes out again with his hands behind his back and nothing on his feet,

'come on kids, youre good at singing, you can sing along with me' he says,

Hey little hen, when, when, when
Will you lay me an egg for my tea?

and Mum always sniffs at his songs but hes got a surprise ready and hes holding it behind his back and now he brings it out and its some stockings,

'nylons! thats such an *extravagance*!' Mum cries out 'Guy, you mustnt!'

but he wont take them back,

'you got these on the Black Market didnt you?' she says,

and now shes angry because the Black Market is a wicked thing, but a good way to make money,

'im a policeman, after all' he says and puts a finger on his lips,

Mum says Guys the man of the house and now its Saturday morning he takes us to the pictures and i get to hold on to my own ticket while we queue up outside the Gaumont for a treat because this is Laurel and Hardy in something with a ladder thats hilarious, and while we wait for the second film i suck on a bullseye and watch newsreels of the war but we already know whats happening because we listen to the BBC, though its different when you can watch soldiers carrying the shells and the big artillery guns firing, and Mr Churchill smiles with a cigar in his mouth while he lifts his hat and makes the V sign so we know Miss Wilkins is wrong because we are going to win,

but when we get home theres nothing to do except play dominoes and stuff in the kitchen because now Guy sleeps in the lounge room we dont go there anymore, not even to tinker with the piano and Mum has stopped singing,

an iron blind rattles down outside the watchmakers and next to that theres a CLOSED sign hanging inside WH Smiths door,

and i plan to walk backwards all the way home just to hold everyone up,

'Rodney!'

somebodys calling my name and im surprised and the others stop to watch because its Mrs Arbuthnot sticking her head out of the bookshop doorway,

'do come back, Rodney' she says,

now it hits me,

she has been lying in wait ever since that day!

'just a moment' she says,

and she ducks inside and the CLOSED sign is flapping,

'run!' i whisper,

'why?' Mike says,

but Diana grabs hold of me to stop me getting away,

'have you been up to mischief?' she says,

'let go of me!' i say,

but already its too late because Mrs Arbuthnots back with a book in her hand,

'whats this?' says Mike,

and i feel my face go red and my eyes fill with tears,

'i didnt do it' i say,

'how any such thing could happen im sure i dont know' Mrs Arbuthnot says 'unless you were carrying your copy when you came in before Christmas'

and i dont know what to say,

she turns to Michael to explain to him,

'apparently we were tidying up' she says 'and we put Rodneys book back in the pile'

something marvellous begins to catch up with me,

'you big ones must see to it that he is more careful in future' she says,

and she puts the Enid Blyton in my hands,

'goodbye' she says,

and back she goes and closes the door on herself, so i hold it out to show my brother and he takes it and opens the front cover and stands for ages reading my name written in my own writing,

'i didnt want Guy to take Mum down to the police station' i say when theres no escape 'thats why i gave it back'

'well if you stole it in the first place youre going to have to throw it away' Mike says,

'not now Mrs Arbuthnot has *given* it to me!' i stamp and scream in the middle of the street till people stop and stare 'and you saw! and she did!'

and Mike pulls a face and tries to shut me up, then he just sticks my book inside his own jumper,

'i dont know why im doing this' he says,

and i like lying down under a tree and looking up at the sky when its blue and listening to see what i can hear, and i dont mind when Miss Wilkins calls me a dreamer only i dont like real dreams much because real dreams are mostly about men with guns stepping out of my bedroom cupboard,

and i need to hurry or Gran might catch me out, because if she doesnt shes never going to guess that im peeing on her beautiful carpet right under this cow picture, and the bathrooms only just upstairs so theres no *reason*, but i want to, and the carpet soaks it up and theres not a thing to be seen so now i shall never be found out,

and i sit on one side of the table and Aunt Olive sits on the other side and in between us is her fruitcake and its still warm and shes jolly and we keep taking slices till weve eaten the whole thing right down to the last crumb,

'there' says Aunt Olive 'so thats that!'

and i call her aunty though she isnt really and she gets up to put a record on a gramophone and *weve* got a gramophone too but ours doesnt work,

'Popeyes sweetheart is called Olive' i tell her,

and she smiles at me and she looks nice,

'do you like the Palm Court Orchestra?' she asks,

and i say 'yes'

so she gets the music going and then she puts her finger on her lips and comes swishing round my side of the table right up close to me,

'shall i tell you a secret?' Olive says,

and the Palm Court Orchestra is playing on the gramophone,

'what?' i ask,

'ssh!' she says 'my old mother is upstairs and she mustnt know' and i can hear that grumpy mother moving about above us 'your Uncle Ralph has promised to marry me'

'but i think hes already got a wife' i say 'in Australia'

'only until his divorce comes through' she says 'then i shall be your real aunty'

and her dress is so tight you can see the corset holding her tummy in, and i let her kiss me and her face powder smells like lots of flowers,

'its our little secret' she says,

and i dont know what to say next,

'how did i get born?' i ask her because shes the one who always answers my questions,

'well we are all the same, pet' Olive says 'we begin as a tiny thing, tiny like one of these crumbs, until we grow big enough to be a baby and then out we come'

'and we start wailing?'

'exactly'

and i jab my finger on to the last crumb of cake on the dish,

'Olive' i ask 'how did everything begin?'

'you mean *everything*, pet?' Olive says,

and i say 'the whole world'

'because God said Let it all begin' Olive says, 'and everything began?'

'exactly'

and i know why Uncle Ralph wants to marry her, but theres footsteps shuffling across the floor above our heads,

'is that child' Mrs Freestone calls down in her cross voice 'still hanging around?'

im colouring in but Di skips around behind my chair to dig me in the back every time she passes,

'a tisket a tasket!' she sings,

'im not going to play' i yell at her 'im never going to play'

Mrs Bolton doesnt mind me talking while she does peoples ironing for them and the laundrys full of steam even on a spring day and shes as fat as Gran only fatter and her white hair is rolled up on top of her head like a loaf of bread going yellow and she talks and she listens and she works hard because theres a huge pile of shirts and blouses,

'one day' she says 'somebody will invent a tap thatll

give me hot water without lighting the fire first'

'we get hot water for the bath' i tell her 'from the gas geyser'

and she crashes the flat-iron back again on the fire and hoists a hot one on to the ironing board where she rubs it with yellow soap and slaps it down along the sleeve shes ironing,

'or an iron that heats itself up' she says,

but i cant help her out and the whole place stinks of burnt soap,

and i run down to thank the postman because hes put a postcard through the slot at the bottom of the stairs but when i pick it up its only a picture of a bridge, and Mum comes down after me and she takes it,

'Sydney Harbour Bridge' she says,

'whats that?'

'its the biggest bridge in the world' she says 'i think'

'so?'

'your Uncle Ralph worked on this bridge when it was being built' she tells me and then turns it over 'Winifred is sending us another food parcel!'

today we dont ask the time because everythings different at the swimming pool when people have their clothes off, and this makes us late so now weve torn it because the suns going down already when we push through the turnstiles to set off for town, but all of a sudden the skys throbbing anyway and the enemy bombers are on their way over,

'wouldnt you know!' says Mike,

'come along!' says Di,

and they start running,

but im not ready because ive got to finish slinging my towel across my back like an Arab on horseback,

'hey, wait a minute!'

but they are halfway up the hill ahead,

'wait!'

and we are *miles* from any air raid shelter and even the Gaumont is quarter of an hour away let alone home,

'wait for me!' i yell,

but they dont even look back and im tired and sunburnt and i cant keep up and my cheeks joggle and they feel chubby and my whole body *bothers* me,

'hey!' i yell,

when i jog to a stop my towel slips off trailing in the dirt and everything is hopeless,

im trapped in the open between the road and a huge stone wall thats too high for anybody to ever climb, even Guy, and the Luftwaffe drones louder and louder so at any minute now theyre going to drop a whole lot of high explosives that nothing can stop and theres no escape, and i want it, yes i *want* to be killed on the spot so those other two will feel guilty when they find out how selfish theyve been,

and im sobbing so much i collide with Michael,

'theres a new plan' Mike says 'we shall head for Grans because its closer'

so he did come to my rescue after all, but im more furious than ever and i hang on to him and im going to drag him down and i wont let him go because hes a traitor and a dirty pig,

'fuck shit poo!' i shriek in his face and im punching him,

but Mike grabs hold of me and growls 'pull yourself together'

and i know he means business, but i dont care,

'i hope a bomb falls right on top of us' i yell at him 'and then youll get killed with me, because i want those Germans to blow us to smithereens!'

but he drags me up the hill just the same,

and still Miss Wilkins teaches us all the things she knows while we are at school because as well as reading we learn to write with real pens but the one im given is so old theres ink stains in the wooden handle and the nib looks a bit bent so when i dip it in the inkwell and start on a letter R it makes a blot straight away,

and im balancing this big bowl of steamy water and ive got to be careful none spills or splashes on the floor,

'put it here on the table, darlin' Gran says to me,

and poor Joans gone white and her eyes look big and her shoulders hunch and she cant breathe,

'a splash of camphor oil should do the trick' Gran says,

'can i do that?' i ask,

'not this time'

and the smell fills her kitchen and Joan gasps with her face in the steam while Gran drapes a towel over her head like a tent,

'deep breath' Gran says 'oh dear, oh dear'

'is she dying?' i whisper so Joan wont hear,

'its nothing but a bout of asthma' says Gran,

'whats it like under there?' i ask,

but Joan just wheezes,

'at least shes past the worst, then!' Gran says,

so i push among the people crowding the kerb, and i push till i pop right out into the gutter, 'whoa!'

theres a truck filling the road and filling the sky thats right on top of me! but im choking and someones dragging me back to safety, and i look round to find its Mr Higgins from the shoe shop and hes got hold of my collar, and the din all around us is terrific,

so i yell at him 'is it the Americans?'

because now i can see along the road and a line of trucks crawling our way stretches all the way down the hill,

'theyve joined the war at last' he says 'and not before time!'

and theres a girl giving me a smile and her hair looks like its on springs and shes counting the vehicles and i know her because shes in my class,

'seventeen, eighteen—' she counts,

then i join in,

'twenty-one, twenty-two—' we chant together,

and soldiers wearing funny-looking caps lean out to grin down at us and theyre suntanned with white teeth, but some have black skin and wave black hands and theyre all enormous and they throw handfuls of chewing gum,

'my mum wont let me have gum because its bad for you' Pam whispers,

'and my mum wont either because its vulgar'

and while we giggle more packets fly through the air and even packets of cigarettes and then a whole bar of chocolate hits me smack on the chest, so now i know we are going to win the war!

'here come the gun-carriers' someone yells,

yes and armoured cars with slanted noses too, and now there are tanks looming our way like *monsters*, huge guns stick out front and they rumble and squeal and their caterpillars chop up the road, and i can feel the ground buzzing under my feet, and on top there are soldiers standing in the open turrets,

'hi ya!' we yell and 'okay buddy!'

and they look happy because they come out of nowhere,

and i watch a man in the street shake his head and a pigeon flies out of his hat.

7

We all sit down at the table and Guy is next to Mum,

'anything new at the office?' he says,

but she just smiles because shes listening to us talk about school and then she gets up to go to the oven,

Guy opens his crackly newspaper,

'that Rommels a damned good soldier if you ask me, Dods' he says,

and Mum takes a big dish of macaroni cheese from the oven to put on the table and she begins doling it out,

'but we beat him' says Mike,

'thats right' says Mum,

and she passes out the plates with food on them and Di gets hers and i get mine,

'but shes got more crunchy brown bits than me' i complain and point at the evidence on Dis plate,

'serve you right' Di says 'because you got most last Sunday'

'did not'

'did'

'shush, you two' Mike tells us and he looks worried for some reason,

and after a while i say 'did not'

Mum lets out a sigh, so Di gives me a glare just to show me what she *wants* to say, and Guy gets busy cutting slices of bread for us all,

'anybody for pepper and salt?' Mike asks and passes it across the table,

so we all start eating and it tastes good,

'did' Di says,

and Mum throws her fork down on her plate,

'this flat' she shouts at Guy 'is too small for five'

but he doesnt seem to understand because he just gives her a little smile,

'sorry' he says,

'we are too cramped' she says 'so the children keep getting on each others nerves'

and you can see her headache has come back,

'sorry' he says again and he seems to want her to be happy,

but then suddenly shes standing up and her chair topples over behind her, and the chair makes a loud noise and shes got a hanky over her mouth and her eyes are wild and shes staring down at Guy,

'what is it, Mum?' Di screams,

and now Guys hand creeps out from under the tablecloth and hes getting to his feet too, but he moves slowly and hes still smiling, though something terrible comes next because Mums whole body swings and she SMACKS him across the face,

'hey!' Guy says,

and he catches her wrist to hold her away from him, but she tugs her hand free and backs off and she stumbles over the fallen chair and then she gets clear and puts the table between them,

'steady on!' Guy says,

and his voice is somehow nice and i reckon this must be a game of catch because he pretends to go one way and then goes the other,

and he says 'hey!' again,

but shes trying to get away,

'are you alright?' he says,

'dont you dare!' she shouts and shes crouching now 'in my own house!'

and shes shaking all over and Mike begins to yell like a maniac and Di screams, but i dont understand and the smell of cooked cheese on my macaroni makes me feel sick, and Mum stands behind me bumping my shoulder,

'Mum!' i say,

and i watch Guy dancing from one foot to the other but when he doubles back theres someones fist that hits out at him and its Mike, but Guy lifts him off his feet and spins him round to shove him out of the way and i think of the hatchet we keep under the sink, but everyones running already so instead i snatch up the little saucepan from the draining board and swing it but it bounces off Guys shoulder,

'temper temper!' he says though he doesnt hit me,

he doesnt hit any of us,

and the worst thing is that hes laughing and it looks like hes having fun and he towers over us all,

'alright, youve made your point' he says to Mum,

and she glares at him like she hates him,

'but you didnt refuse the nylon stockings' he says,

so he gives up and thats the end of that because he strolls off into the lounge room and sits down at the piano to tinkle some keys, and suddenly Mum rushes after him,

'get out of my house' she shouts 'before i report you to your senior officer!'

and she slams the door on him to shut him away in the lounge,

ive woken in the night because someones moving about in the kitchen and theres a crack of light under the door and i can hear bare feet coming our way across the lino,

'Mike!' i whisper,

but theres no answer, so Mikes asleep and theres just the slash of light and our cupboard in the corner,

now the door opens and the lights too bright, but ive already seen that its Guy standing there looking in and i dont dare breathe in case i give myself away, and while im pretending to be asleep anything at all could happen so im ready to jump up and run and its not the German parachuter im afraid of now, and though my eyes are shut tight i can tell the light is still on and i keep my breathing slow and steady,

it all goes dark again,

i take a peep but i cant see a thing except the kitchen light is off and i dont know if Guy is in there still, or maybe in here,

but ive never heard of such a thing as invisible ink!

'then watch this' says Mike,

and he dips his nib into the little bottle and gets busy writing *nothing* on the piece of paper and he writes with his left hand like he always does, though i think this looks back-to-front, and especially because hes doing the joined-up writing they learn at big school,

'thats it!' he says,

'what?' i say,

because theres nothing on the page,

‘just watch’ he says,

and he strikes a match and lights a candle and he holds the paper just above the candle flame,

‘hey presto!’ says Mike the Magician,

and i cant believe my eyes because words begin to happen on the page, appearing all by themselves,

‘so now’ Mike says to me ‘i can write my biggest secrets and nobody will ever know!’

i *only ever pretend to be good,*

and im watching the fag in the corner of Mabel Greenwoods mouth because ive got a bet on when itll burn her lips,

‘i should trot along’ Mabel says to Mum ‘but its begun teeming’

and Mabel is Mums friend who comes over to play cards,

Mum says ‘im sure Rod could dig out a spare umbrella for you’

so down the dark end of the passage i go and get busy sorting among coats and things hung on our hat-and-coat stand,

'and darling!' Mum calls to me 'find some galoshes for Mabel while youre there!'

but what i find is a *door* behind the coats where it must have been all the time, but when i reach up to give the rusty knob a twist it doesnt work,

'got them' i sing out,

and i cover the door again because this must be a secret escape,

'thanks pet lamb' Mabel sniffles and takes the galoshes from me 'i should have known to bring my own brolly, at least'

'okay' i say 'its okay'

'i do wish you wouldnt use that American slang' Mum says,

but i slip off to share my news with Mike,

'what is it?' Mike says 'i cant hear you, you idiot, if you keep whispering'

so i say out loud 'theres a *door!* along there'

'of course theres a door along there, everyone knows that! and it has to be kept locked because of the staircase behind it'

i say 'but i bet you cant guess where it *goes*!'

because i reckon it may be our way out,

'i dont need to guess' he says and sticks his nose back in his book 'it leads down into the garage workshop'

but that's daft! whats the point of keeping the door

hidden? everybody already knows about the garage underneath us,

'dont worry, Dods' says Mabel trying out our umbrella and getting ready to face the rain 'Guy wont dare come back now'

Pam asks,

'whats your opinion about God?'

'how do you mean?'

'about God saving us and the King as well?'

'i dont know' i tell her because i dont,

and she gets a good look at me,

'do you say your prayers at night?' she says,

'only when im at my Grans place'

'what do you pray for?'

'money'

'is that all?'

'and melon and lemon jam'

'well i think youre a little sinner' she says 'thats what i think'

and i dont mind, though somehow ive got to find out about God saving *me* but if i ask Gran shes bound to take me to church and thatll waste a whole Sunday,

and theres no one else at home so now its safe to open up Mums cabinet where she keeps her treasures and i poke around inside, but the lid of her cigarette tins stuck, so i have to hug it against my chest to get a grip,

'there!'

and sure enough the photographs are safe inside so i take one out and its the picture of Mum beside the ant-hill but im not going to put it back, so i pop the rest away again and snap the tin shut and close the cabinet door,

but no! wait a minute! fingerprints on the tin! quick! i use a handkerchief to pick it up and i rub it against my pants! and Mum wont notice because ive only taken one photo,

still, i go into the bathroom and bolt the door in case anyone comes home early and i sit on the lavatory to get a good look and heres the ant-hill that the giant ants made at Kangaroo Valley on the farm,

'are we allowed?' i ask,

'shut up and stay in the shadow of the wall' Mike whispers 'so no one can see you!'

but im already squashed right up close to it and squatting under the TRESPASSERS WILL BE PROSECUTED sign,

'whats prosecuted, Mike?'

'chased and caught' he says,

and the terror jumps out at me, like theres big men in hats all rushing to catch us, but Mike still gives the signal to slip round the side of the tower while nothings there except some scraps of old yellow paper blowing across the yard,

'why—?' i say,

'shut up and follow me!' says Mike,

and we trample the weeds growing in the cracks at the bottom of the wall,

'do people work here?' says Di,

'not anymore' Mike says 'its abandoned'

'my knees bleeding' i say,

'that doesnt matter' Mike says,

the sky passes behind the tower so the whole thing seems to be falling on top of us,

'we could have gone down to the canal instead' i complain 'and we could be having a good time'

but Mikes found some kind of hatch that hes looking for and he gets out the spike on his penknife and sets to work on the clip,

'whats Mum going to say when she hears?' i say,

'we *should* be able—' Mike says,

'bad luck its rusted' i say to annoy him,

but something snaps and he gasps, and now hes holding the rusty flap open,

'so its a square hole' i say,

'and not very big' Di says,

but when Mike wriggles in she wriggles in too and so do i and the heavy flap swings shut behind me,

'so dark!' Dis voice says,

CLANG goes something and i hold my breath because a whole lot of light swamps down on us,

'we seem to be at the bottom' says Mike 'this is some kind of outlet thing'

'how do we get through?' Di says,

and Mike turns to me 'youre the smallest'

'i wont go' i say,

but he gives me a leg up anyway, and i worm and i squirm till im over the shelf at the top,

'what can you see?' Di asks,

'WOW! youll never guess!' i say,

'what?'

'the whole place is white!' i say,

'but what can you *see*?' says Mike,

'its all air!'

'but whats it *like*?' Diana demands,

'you can see everything' i explain,

'but WHAT?' says Mike,

'its empty' i tell them because i can look up as high as high 'and theres chains hanging down' i tell them 'chains and hooks'

and they start scrambling through and Mikes head comes up out of the hole 'so much *sunlight*!' he says,

and he stands beside me and pats me on the back and Dis last and shes banging dust off her frock,

'whys the floor white?' she says,

and i dig some *flour* from between the boards,

'look!' i say,

'flour in a flour mill' Mike says 'so what?'

and Di spreads her arms and flies,

'is this the biggest place ever built?' she says,

'dont be a dope' Mike says,

'what if it falls down?' i say,

and something gives a quiet *clunk* and another *clunk* and a soft *boom*,

'lets get out!' i whisper,

'its just the wind!' Mike says,

the same *boom* happens again but in all this enormous space i cant see a single thing that could make such a noise,

'see?' says Mike,

'see *what*?' i yell at him and the echo comes back at us *OTTTTtttt*,

and Mike puts a finger to his lips till it dies away,

'the whole place is made of tin!' Di says 'its painted tin'

and she darts across the bare floor with her plaits flying,

'YEAH!' Mike shouts *YYYYEEEEEEEEEEEEEEEE EEEEEEEyeyeyeyeye yeyeaaaaaaah*, and i hit and hit him,

'shut your gob!' i yell *OOBbbbbb*

'the air stinks in here' Di says from over her side,

Mike calls 'its because im sending poison gas your way!'

and he makes a farting noise with his mouth,

i start laughing and now im walking backwards across the floor so i can see everything back-to-front and i keep on going right up the stairs step by step to the first landing,

'im King George!' i yell *ORRrrrgggge*,

and i wave down at the others,

Di claps her hands and she calls out 'i bags General Montgomery'

but Mike tells her 'youre a *girl* so youve got to be a nurse'

and i drop down on my good knee to take a pot-shot at him between the rails because this is an *ambush*, but Mike makes his getaway racing past us and climbing so high up that he reaches the upstairs rooms that stand open,

'whats there, Mike?' i call,

'nothing'

and now he swings from a big hook with his legs going like a bicycle, so i get him in my sights and my machine-gun does the trick,

'youre dead!' i yell,

and now we are hiding and we go everywhere on tiptoe and nobody can see anybody, and i crouch down to take cover and in this corner theres a ledge where i find a chipped cup with a brown stain inside and a few dry tea leaves at the bottom, and everythings gone quiet so i take out my stolen photograph of Kangaroo Valley to prop against the cup and get a good look, and i remember Joan telling us about a black dog called Rose that had to be left behind when they came to England and she loved Rose, so maybe Rose is still waiting for her to come home because there was even a dog that walked right across England to find his owners because it was on the news,

but Dis already ducking along the catwalk so i catch up and now its a race to the top,

'dare you' says Di,

'dare you' i say,

and we have to count the steps we tramp up and we count to a hundred and twenty-one but now i cant look down or else im going to fall,

'are you two being stupid?' Mike yells *PIDDDDdddddd*,

'dont look down' Di tells me,

so i do, and the whole building starts to tilt and i cant hang on and i let go but suddenly Michaels here and i dont know where he came from but hes got hold of me and helps me to sit on a ledge,

'take your time' he says 'to get over the giddiness'

'i want to go home' i say,

'alright' he says 'but first weve got to get to the top'

and he leads the way till we get up right into a sort of turret thing thats so small there isnt room to stand properly,

'this ventilator is just for letting the air out' he says,

but what i can feel is air coming *in* because all round us the slats are fixed at the same angle and i can see the town far down below and tiny people walking around the streets,

'storm coming in from the west' Mike warns and he points,

and we watch the clouds glide our way and some rain streaks past and the grey roofs down there go black while dinky vans move this way and that and umbrellas open and everythings shiny,

'now that we know where west is' Mike says 'we can set up the other directions'

'so which way is Kangaroo Valley?' i ask,

Mike takes a marble from his pocket and holds it between his finger and thumb,

'watch!' he says,

and he drops it so we watch it fall and fall and fall,

'that way' he says,

and it bounces at the bottom, *tak, tak, tak, tak tak tak-tak,*

'okay' Mike says and he starts down 'the wars on again'

and now hes running along the catwalk and dodging

into empty offices and ive got him in my sights and when my bullets hit him he staggers and falls against the railing,

'i was on a secret mission' he gasps,

'thats sabotage' Di explains,

'but im dying a heros death' he says,

'lets hide again then' i say,

but Mike finds the opening to a thing that slopes down and hes already peering inside it,

'theres a chute here' he says,

we go to look inside it too but its nothing but a huge square tube,

'whys it so shiny?' Di asks,

'because millions and millions of grains of wheat polished it' Mike says,

'thats silly' says Di 'you polish things with a *cloth*'

and i hang over to look

'its empty' i say and my voice is like a head in a bucket,

'this can be our emergency tunnel' Mike says,

and we watch him sit on the edge and then he slides all the way down the slope and hes gone,

'Mike?'

but his face appears at the bottom and hes laughing up at us,

'is it safe?' Di says,

'have a go' he says, all boomy,

'me first' i say,

and suddenly im away because my bottom gets whisked from under me so that i fall flat on my back and i have to slide down like that the whole way because i cant sit up again but Mike catches me when i come out like a bullet and i roll on to the floor,

'i know why its called a shoot!' i yell *OOOoooootttttt*,

'ssh!' Mike says 'because we are escaped prisoners of war and with any luck this tunnel might lead us under the barbed-wire entanglements'

and we run on tiptoe in between big rusty machines till we can wriggle into that rusty hatch we found at the beginning when we came up through it and we are in the dark again until Mike swings the flap open so we can crawl out into the rain,

'are we going to come back again tomorrow and play in here forever?' i ask,

'just shut up and stay near the wall' Mike says 'and keep out of sight!'

and now we are trespassers again,

though we are back at home and out of the rain my heads still full of the empty flour mill and even while we stamp our feet and dump our wet things in the kitchen im thinking about the echoes and im planning a new plan for next time, and Mums at the piano singing 'i attempt from loves sickness to fly'

so we troop in to join her and we sing along because we know all her favourites, and theres no need to worry about whether it means anything because the words go with the music,

'i attempt from loves sickness to fly-y-y-y in vain, since i am myself my own fever, since i am myself my own fever and pain'

and i sing the loudest 'FE-EV-VER A-AND PAIN' because Mum must never find out that weve been trespassing at the flour mill or shes sure to stop us going back there,

Mikes the king with all the gold and im going to get it off him,

im leaning against Di and shes leaning against me because weve already got the giggles and it all started with the parson speaking through his nose, or maybe the giggles began when Gran told us that the hard seat is called a pew and we said 'oh pew!' at the same time, and to make matters worse someone sitting behind us has the collywobbles, and now Gran glares at us and she smacks Dis knee but thats funny too and im going to EXPLODE,

'why do ye not understand my speech?' says the parson looking sideways at the Bible hes reading out of because his nose gets in the way and sounding very cross,

oh help!

'ye are of your Father the Devil' he says,

and the spit flies and he wags his long wrinkly finger,

but my howl of laughter is awful as well,

'you wicked, wicked' Gran hisses,

and she drags me by the hand and Di too,

'you wicked children!' she hisses,

and we stumble along the aisle, both of us doubled up and limping while that nosy voice drones on till the thick old door swings shut behind us and we stagger down some steps into the drizzle,

'i was never so disgraced' says Gran,

and i know shes serious because she doesnt bother about her hat getting wet,

but i have to stay at home because Dianas caught the mumps and shes sick in bed and Doctor Halliday came and said im not allowed to go to school till she gets better because maybe ive caught it too and Mum says mumps is dangerous for boys but not for girls though i dont know why, and now im BORED with trying to get a stupid game of patience to work out but it wont, not even when i cheat, and im sick of our train set because ive finished playing with that and ive already built the tallest tower out of the meccano and stuck it away in a corner and ive done a galleon drawing with wind in its sails and ive gone through all my Popeyes and Beanos and theres *nothing* left to do, so i take a peek in at the bedroom door to see how Dianas doing,

'are you going to die?'

'shut up you beast!' she says,

and shes crying so i leave her,

and what wakes me is a dream, i was having a dream about Guy because he had his shirt off and he was lying on his back and somehow i was rolling on his chest,

and Di got over the mumps but now Mum feels ill and shes the one who stays in bed but i dont reckon its a cold or the flu or anything like that because of how quiet she is, and when i come out of the bedroom i show the others the money Mum just put in my hand,

'i think its a migraine' i report to Mike and we know

this is the biggest sort of headache of all,

'so much money!' he says,

'thats not for you!' Di says,

'its the rent' i tell them,

and Mike takes it off me 'ten-and-sixpence' he says,

'Mum says we are to stick it in an envelope' i say,

and now i know what it feels like to be rich,

so out we go downstairs to call on the landlord in his garage and no one can stop us and we march right in though weve never been allowed past the petrol pumps, and because weve got money the garage men let us walk right in among the cars waiting to be filled and theres a *bus* too with a missing wheel and theres a man making sparks explode and his voice comes from behind the mask he wears,

'oy! keep clear, you brats!'

and he waves us away and Mike points up above us because we are directly underneath our yard and i get a look at some sunny clouds through the skylight, and a mechanic in overalls points to the manager sitting in his office with bunches of papers hanging on the wall and hes so surprised to see us he snatches his cap off his head and throws it down on his work,

'what the hell!' he roars,

'Mums ill' Mike says 'so we are the ones to bring the rent'

and the manager calms down and scratches his head,

'well, thats alright then' he says 'but the workshop is no place for youngsters like you'

and im looking at some coloured pictures of ladies in bathers stuck to the glass,

'its not safe' he says,

and he counts the money and licks his fingers to flick through the pages in his receipt book and then licks his fingers again so he can pick up the little piece of blue carbon paper for slipping in at the right place before he gets busy writing,

'thank you' says Mike,

but i get a sick feeling in my tummy because weve given him all that money,

'and now id better see you safely out' says the manager,

and he leads the way showing us around while an old man comes wriggling out from underneath a three-wheeler van to peer at us through very thick glasses and he puffs at the last bit of a cigarette stuck to his lip,

'my best mechanic' he tells us,

and Mike says 'our Uncle Dick Riney has a Railton Special'

'lucky him' says the mechanic and coughs a whole lot of smoke and rummages in his overalls to pull out a snotty old handkerchief that he spits into,

the manager shows us a dark corner 'those stairs lead up to your place' he says, but all there is is a closed door at the top of some dusty steps with old junk and telephone books stacked on them,

'that doors never opened' says Mike,

'on our side weve got it hidden behind a hat-and-coat stand' Di explains,

'and its got bolts on it' i say,

'just make sure to thank your mother for me' says the manager to Di because shes the one he gives the receipt to,

'i feel better now the last of Guys money has been paid over' Mum tells us and she tries to smile,

so i throw myself on her bed and i cry and cry while she strokes my hair,

'what is it?' she says,

but Mike says 'hes just an idiot'

Joan gives me and Di a couple of Horlicks tablets and we get busy sucking them,

'wallabies' she says 'are small kangaroos that raid your kitchen garden'

'what for?' i ask,

'so they can bite off every scrap of spinach right down to the roots'

'spinach is my favourite' i say and the reason is a secret,

but Joan doesnt remember Mums ant-hill.

'Mum says im a horror the way i talk' i say,

'yes youre a horror and an urchin' Joan says,

and shes a teacher who teaches elocution so our problem can be fixed,

'but whats wrong with slang?' i say 'i like slang'

'now youre coming for lessons you have to do as i tell you' Joan says,

and i will because i love her and she laughs and she has the whitest teeth of anybody because she brushes them with pink tooth powder, so she gives me a biscuit and some ginger pop and kisses me and afterwards im allowed out in the garden to throw a ball for her scottie dog while Di has her lesson, but i run back indoors to the drawing room instead to look at that oil painting of the cows,

and what i want to tell you is that ive got a plan and im going to run away from home,

and i like watching Mrs North mixing Grans medicine for her indigestion that we are going to take back to her, and Michael is buying chemist stuff off old Mr North for his chemistry experiments,

'and some sulphur, please' Mike says 'and saltpetre too'

and old Mr North shakes the powders into separate little paper cones and hes very careful,

'dont forget a new test tube' i say because Mike told me to remind him,

and Mr North holds up some test tubes to show us the different sizes hes got and we can see through the glass with him looking at us,

Mike teaches us how to whistle but nothing comes out except air and i try and try and Dianas trying too and she goes red in the face, and i hate this now and its got to be because hes showing us wrong so i give up, but right at the end of my breath a little hint of a whistle happens, super! and now i know i can do it so im going to practise every single day of my life till i can whistle Clementine and tunes like that,

'good try' says Mike,

and he gives a wolf-whistle,

'thats what you want to be able to do' he tells me 'so you can do it at girls'

'okay' i say,
and i will,
'but what about me?' says Di,
he thinks about it,
'girls dont do wolf-whistles' he says,

and i ask 'are we in the gang now?'

and even the fat kid sneers at me, but weve started hanging round with them,

'snakes are weird' the fat boy says 'and your brothers weird'

because theyve come to the woods with us to hunt for pet snakes and Michaels already caught a grass snake that gives off an awful stink and we all stand watching it coil around his fist,

'Uuurgghh!' the fat boy says,

and the others start staggering and making sick noises, but Mike doesnt care because he knows what hes doing and he flicks the snake into the bag we brought,

'Arthur died' i explain 'when i was little'

'lets get going' says one kid,

and we set off walking across some flat rocks while the bag wriggles,

'anyhow' says the big boy with a split lip 'what i was sayin about tarts—'

'yes' says another 'and out on the common is where you go to pick up the leavings'

'i know about tarts' i tell them 'theyre ladies who go into telephone booths'

'first thing of a morning' one boy tells me 'when you go for a walk—'

'—*and* if you look' the fat one says,

'—then you find the puffballs of white stuff the soldiers leave behind'

'but how do you mean *puffballs*?' i ask,

and he says 'well i spose theyre more like little balloons, you know?'

and yes, i do know because i get a picture of balloons as small as mushrooms filled with white powder,

'so why do the soldiers leave them behind?' Mike asks,

and the kids in the gang start falling about all stupid and *collapsing* against each other and yelling and happy and making us feel stupid,

because Mums feeling fine she digs out an old hat with feathers on it and walks around town with the feathers fluttering, so thats how we all feel and we hold hands and this is new and we stop to look into every single shop window there ever was and we play *i spy with my little eye* and we even play double *i spy* and this is hilarious, and mine at the green grocers is 'terrible turnip' and Di at the hobby shop gets 'dopey dominoes', we all laugh and people stare and we laugh louder and we *i spy* at Woolworths Penny Stores and we *i spy* at Lewises frock shop and Mum gives us 'b' at the photographers but we have to give in because we cant get it and its 'bumptious bride' and i think bumptious is the funniest thing i ever heard and its my word now and Mike gets 'crazy corsets' at the ladies underwear shop and Mum laughs so much she has to find a handkerchief to save her make-up,

and out of town we pass rows of houses with little front gardens and Mum tells us the names of the flowers so we can learn and people smile at us because we smile at them, and they can see our picnic basket but they dont know whats in it or that we get sent jam and things from Australia and they dont know im going to sail right around the world so i can sit by a camp fire and ride a horse,

'we shall borrow some rugs from Gran to spread on her lawn' Mum says,

so thats the plan,

and going down Grans hill i get to skid in the gravel because its so steep,

'think of your shoes!' Mum says,

and i know its wrong,

'but i cant stop' i say,

and the hedges are jumping around and stones go

flying and the stream glitters down there and the woods beyond Grans place zoom closer and the high stone wall around her garden too,

'Rod!' Mike warns me 'those shoes of yours are new!'

but thats whats so good and YOW! i skid in among some nettles at the side of the track,

'serve you right' he says,

but i dont want him to know how much it stings so i get busy rubbing my legs with the dock leaves ive found,

Mike starts picking up stones and chucking them over the hedge,

'theres Joan' Di shouts,

and Joan is standing at the open door and she comes down into the garden and she seems to be in a rush and now shes running along the drive towards us,

'maybe we cant have the picnic after all' Mike says,

and she rushes up to Mum and her face is all red and streaky and she throws her arms around her,

'what is it dear?' Mum says 'what can it be?'

and Joan cant get her breath,

'm-my scottie is gone!' she blubbers,

'he ran away?' Mum asks.

'i was out and—' Joan blubbers,

'—and when i got home' Joan blubbers,

'he was—' Joan tries again,

and Gran has come to stand in the doorway up ahead and though shes still a long way off i can already see shes looking grim,

‘i *told* her’ Gran calls out for us to hear and she stands there ‘so the vet was sent for’

and her voice sounds tiny and terrible,

but what *happened*? i kind of know though i dont understand and i begin wailing for the puppy and Di joins in,

Mum straightens her hat and leads the march up to the house,

‘but what got into you?’ Mum snaps,

and shes snapping at her mother just like she snaps at us when weve been naughty, and while Gran is usually so soft and plump shes not like that now,

‘and i shant have you answer back, Doris’ Gran says ‘i shall not put up with it’

‘but how *could* you?’ Mum says,

and i show Gran my tears so she will understand but her round face is all set and hard,

‘such a dear little dog’ Joan wails,

‘a *dear little dog*!’ Gran turns indoors ‘i could tell you a thing or two! the stinking thing!’ and she bangs the door shut behind her,

leaving us outside on the drive holding our picnic basket,

Mrs Harris at the Railway Hotel does her washing out in the yard and we lend a hand because we like her and because she talks about all sorts of things and i watch her in all the heat and steam dipping a pole into the big copper and she drags out a sheet thats so long and wet and heavy its never going to end and she grumbles about what a terrible lot of trouble she has to put up with from the soldiers staying there,

'and i dont have a choice because theyre *billeted*' she says,

'we had Guy billeted on us' i tell her 'but Mum got rid of him'

'so i hear' Mrs Harris laughs,

and Di and i get hold of the hot sheet and begin twisting it end-to-end till water splashes round our feet with bits of suds and big bubbles that turn different colours in the light,

'good girl' Mrs Harris says to Diana and just because shes her favourite she says 'girls are better at wringing than boys'

so i drop my end of the sheet in the dirt,

my feet are cold and i cant do anything or even think,

we are busy sucking Oxo soup cubes and mine tastes good though it only cost a farthing and farthings are my favourite, not because of King George but because of the perky little wren on the other side, and we are tramping through the park,

'lets sit on that bench' Di says,

and right there we find a key that someone must have lost and its one of those little flat front door keys,

'its for a Yale lock' Mike says and he goes through the whole bunch of keys he carries around looking for one like it,

'how many have you got?' i ask and im jealous,

'four Yales' he says 'and theyre all different'

'how many altogether?'

'seventeen and i bags this one too'

'thats not fair' says Di,

and its not,

but because he loves keys he keeps it and im going to have keys of my own when i get big and im going to put them on a key ring so they can jingle when i run,

i hear the back door open because Mum always leaves early on Saturdays and then she has her half-day off in the afternoon, but this time i hear a cry of surprise so i get busy huffing on our bedroom window to thaw the frost and see out, and Mike comes over and kneels on my bed with me,

and what we see is the whole yard covered with *ice* right into the corners so it fits like a carpet,

and it glimmers,

'so much ice!' i say,

and Mum is already on her way out, all dolled up in her old fur-collar overcoat,

'with multiplication tables' Mike explains 'you can estimate how many tons of it weve got out there'

and in her high heels Mum goes *teetering* across like shes learning to fly with her arms stretched out to balance her,

but—

she skids a bit, but—

she reaches the door at the top of the stairs and grabs hold of the handle and she turns our way to wave,

'is she *saying* something?' i ask,

but its too far to hear because our windows shut,

and Mike shrugs at me and i shrug at him so we jump off the bed together and race outside on to the step but we dont dare tread on the ice because its slippery like glass and as big as the swimming baths at Stratford Park,

'*what?*' i yell out to her,

'can you boys please clear a path' Mum calls back 'through the ice?'

'okay' we say together, but it sounds American, so then we both say 'alright'

and down the stairs she goes till its only her bobbing hat and then nothing, while Mike and i stand side by side to look the job over, him with his head on one side so he can judge the job,

'its too big' i say,

'soon we are going to be men' he corrects me 'and men work'

'and i like work' i say changing sides,

'so what we do is to make a start'

and we shut the back door to keep the warmth in and rush for the bedroom to pull some woollies on and we rush down the corridor to fetch our Wellies and i bang on Mums bedroom door to wake Diana on the way,

'youll never guess!' i yell,

and i go out and show her and i lie down on the ice so im first to try it out,

'i wish it would snow too' i say,

and i roll over on my tummy like a swimmer,

'have you gone crazy?' Mike laughs and comes skidding over,

'oooh!' Di sings out from the open doorway,

'watch me' i say,

'youre such a nincompoop!' she says,

and i wriggle like a newt, so now she steps out all gingerly and gets down on her tummy too and wriggles up to me and its a wriggling *race*, but Michael glides there and back while standing up,

'its our own slide!' he says as he slithers to a stop,

'dare you!' i say to Di,

'dare you!' Di says to me,

so we both try taking a run at it like him but our gumboots get in the way and Di falls over and now shes going to cry and spoil everything but she sees the funny side instead,

'hey!' Mike shouts and now hes showing off,

and he whizzes past both our skylights, right to the head of the stairs and i can see that hes going to crash because hes moving too fast to stop so hes bound to trip over the sill and tumble all the way down to the bottom and break his neck,

'ta-ra!' he shouts

because he grabs the doorpost at the last moment and he spins around grinning at us and his scarfs dangling lopsided so he has to hook it over his shoulder,

'my turn' i say,

and i try again but my cap falls off and when i make a grab for it i collide with Di and we both fall in a heap and our coats are covered in frost and Dis got frost on the tip of her nose,

'*weve* invented the best way to keep warm' she shouts at Mike,

so when we help ourselves to breakfast the kitchen

is *fuggy* with fumes after Mum left the paraffin heater on for us and the frost starts melting on our clothes and we scoop some porridge into bowls and sprinkle it with brown sugar and make plans for that path across the yard so Mum can be safe when she comes home and Michael sticks our dirty bowls in the sink, and all of us clump about in boots and wrap scarves round our necks again and pick up some tools and tramp outside, Mike has the spade and we have the little coal shovels,

'okay, watch this' he says and he walks backwards using the spade to scratch a line on the ice 'the shortest way between two points is a straight line'

and thats the sort of thing you learn when youre thirteen,

'Di starts working outside the kitchen door' Mike tells us 'i start at the other end and, Rod, you start in the middle right here beside this skylight'

and i rub a bit of the skylight clear so i can look through the glass down into the garage below, and now im all ready to get cracking because my knees are bare and theyre too cold even though i pull my socks up as high as theyll go,

'is it a race?' i ask,

'no' he says 'its a proper job'

but i clap my mittens together because it *is* a race if you ask me and ive got a secret weapon in my pocket and its the screwdriver from the kitchen cupboard that no one knows about, so i hunch over and get to work and the knack is to chip the ice in a straight line till bits begin breaking off like stars, so i reckon im winning because Dis back there huffing and puffing and i can just imagine her gritting her teeth the way she does,

'this ice is so hard!' she grumbles,

but i keep at it with my screwdriver until i break right through the slab and i chip a trench thats long enough to get the shovel in with the blade under the edge of the ice,

'this slab must be *two inches* thick!' Mike calls 'and thats tons of ice!'

and hes right because my shovels no use and i prove it when the ice wont break and im so furious i stamp on the handle of the stupid thing, *whack*!

'hooray!'

because a big plate of ice *snaps* off and skids to one side leaving splintered bits around the hole that look like toytown cliffs so i get the idea of popping back indoors to fetch my Dinky tractor to play with and my Dinky tip-truck too perhaps, so i stick the secret screwdriver in my pocket because i dont want Michael finding out or he will grab it off me because i know him,

'hey!' i shout,

and i scramble to my feet,

'what?' Mike says and looks up,

so i hold the chunk of ice to show him and i plonk one boot on the skylight because im the champion—

and the—

yard swoops—

smacks me in the face,

and im—

winded!

flat out on the ice and—

theres a sharp pain in my *mouth* and my cheek burns because im flat on my face and theres one dagger of ice with a blob of blood on it,

Michael yanks me up,

'how can anyone cut his tongue' he yells at me 'against the *ground*?'

'nnngg'

'how?' Mikes shouting right in my face,

'nnngg'

'let your tongue hang out' he says 'so we can get a proper look'

'nnngg'

and he gets a look and says 'youve slit it right open'

and Di comes to take a look too,

and she says 'youre like a dying duck in a thunderstorm'

'and now youve got to stay out here and drip on the ground till i come back' Mike says 'and dont get any blood on your coat'

but next thing hes opened a big square biscuit tin that he shoves against my chest to show me how to hold it because he says i can go back indoors now as long as i catch every drop of blood, so i hug the tin close and Mike gets behind me to steer me by the shoulders,

'dont slip again' he warns and we tread carefully,

'mind the step' he says,

but i cant see it because the biscuit tins in the way so i stumble,

'didnt i tell you!' he says,

but he helps me and sits me near the paraffin heater in the kitchen,

'get as close as possible' he says 'to keep warm'

its all very well for him but my tongue *hurts* and what worries me is that he cant work out how to stop the bleeding and he wont even give me an aspirin for the pain because he says i mustnt swallow anything in case i swallow my tongue too and all i can think of is losing my tongue down inside my tummy and never being able to get it out again,

'and make sure you dont suffocate to death' he says 'or Mum will be cross'

and he orders Di to get on with the work outside while he stays inside with me and reads out loud from the Enid Blyton book, and all through the story my tongue is throbbing so i cant think about anything else but i let the story happen just the same and when its finished i crouch close over the heater and shake my head to tell him not to stop,

'what, more?' he says and sighs,

so he goes on to read the newspaper but thats not about anything, just the Russians this and the Germans that and the Americans—

and here comes Mum at last and she drops her bag and lets out a scream because of all this blood swilling about in the biscuit tin, but ive been expecting her *all day* and im not going to cry so i look up through my eyebrows and watch her over the top of the tin,

'and then he—' Mike tells the tale,

but while she listens she gets her handkerchief and folds it into a strip that she wraps around my tongue and then she stuffs the corners inside my cheeks and makes me gag,

'—on the skylight frame, Mum' Mike says 'and the ice and the slope—'

'he fell down on his face!' Di explains 'whack!'

'nnggg' i say,

'and hes been here all morning and ive been looking after him' Mike says,

'and ive had to do all the *work*' Di says,

'—he cut it on the broken ice' Mike says 'only because his mouth was open and he never shuts up'

'well thank you, dear' Mum says to him 'now youre in charge of rinsing this blood down the drain'

and she asks me if i can stand up alright, and once i do she buttons up my jacket and turns me round on the spot and guides me out of doors with my tongue tied up in that handkerchief and what i see is Diana still down on her hands and knees chipping at the ice and the path is still not even half done,

'here we go, young fella-me-lad' Mum says to cheer me up and we step into the stairwell,

and i know she thinks i shall smile at this, though i dont feel like it and i cant anyway, and so we go down and down and my Wellington boots and her shoes make lots of noise because we get in each others way and i keep bumping against the iron wall while im wonky, and out in the lane our shoulders brush against the bricks and Mums stooping and walking lopsided so she can help me along,

'whats he staggering for?' the fish-shop lady asks,

and im always afraid Mumll get talking to her and find out about that lie,

'i cant carry him' Mum tells her 'since hes grown too big'

and the fish-shop lady waves to us as we set off up the street and i try not to look at my feet because that makes me giddy, but whats worse is an RAF officer watching us, so now i look stupid in front of everyone,

i tug at her to get her to cross the street,

'try not to lean against my leg, darling' Mum says 'youll trip me'

safely over and heading towards the clock tower but it sways and the whole town is swaying and the RAF man charges my way and he must think he knows us or something but i never saw him before, and now his arms are around me and im dropping and zooming up again like a ferris wheel and held against his shoulder and i never felt anything so enormous as his arm muscles, and his chest rumbles because hes saying something to Mum and i can feel it all through my body, so now i dont care about anything and i dont care about my *tongue* and im not even listening because all i can feel is his rumbling chest and i see the telephone booth sway past beyond his blue collar, and now we are at Mr Norths chemist shop with those huge bottles of red and purple water in the window, and Guy never held me like this and i can smell the airmans uniform and its so good i burrow in,

'i hope you wont get blood on you' Mum says to him,

and he holds me away a bit, but i look up to show him my tongue in the handkerchief and then i cant help myself because i have to do it, i reach out to touch his moustache,

'he has lost such a lot of blood' Mum says,

'*i* had that' the airman says right into my face 'when i was wounded by flak'

so hes got real war wounds and now this is something i know about him that no one else knows except Mum,

'we are nearly there' Mum says 'the hospitals only just up the road a bit'

and i feel like crying now, but i dont dare let any tears show, ‘we are so very grateful’ Mum tells him when we climb the steps ‘may i ask if youre a pilot?’

‘no, madam, only a humble navigator’

‘im sure that my brother’ Mum says to him ‘is doing his bit for the war, too’

‘you must be proud’ he says ‘what service is he in?’

but i *know* stuff about navigators and compasses and maps that i could tell him if only my tongue was working,

‘hes a good lad’ he tells Mum while he joggles me like a friend and watches my eyes, and i smell the smoke on his breath ‘he can take it’

and this gives me the idea that maybe i *can* take it and its a new idea that i want to think about,

and we go in and the navigator puts me down on a chair and a nurse takes charge of me,

‘wave goodbye, darling’ Mum tells me ‘our friend is leaving’

but i wont wave because i wont say goodbye,

‘no’ i say,

and i cant believe hes such a traitor and he goes,

‘how *could* you!’ she hisses ‘how could you embarrass me so!’

and she reaches out to straighten my school cap and we watch him open the glass door and he walks away,

‘when hes such a nice man’ Mum says,

and she calls out to him ‘goodbye and thank you’

so i feel bad,

'good luck' the navigator calls back and turns our way so he can smile and hes still holding the door,

'you are so rude' she tells me and shes still waving 'and he was so kind carrying you'

but i can still feel his voice rumbling in my body and its a new thing,

'well now you have to be brave for the doctor' Mum says,

and already a nurse unwraps my tongue and she stuffs some bandage in my mouth instead,

'tst *tst*!' she says,

and there are other people in the waiting room,

'boys will be boys' the nurse says to Mum 'i shall take him through to the ward'

and now the nurse picks me up, just like that, and cradles me in her arms so that i hate her more, and along the shiny passage we go, with her so huge and soft and warm and im *suffocating* and much as i wriggle she holds me so its like fighting to get out from under pillows and anyway what makes it worse is that i suddenly realise theres something i need to ask for but i cant talk with this bandage round my tongue, and already the nurse has me on a bed and shes tucking me in and strapping the sheet tight, but this is wrong, and i know because i need the lavatory and i need to ask where it is and how long im supposed to be here before they let me get up, but theres a gag stuffed in my mouth, 'tst *tst*!' she says when i struggle,

so why doesnt somebody tell me what they are going to do to me!

'stay' she says,

i try to tell her my problem 'nngg'

'you are *not* to get out of bed till doctor gives permission' she says 'do you hear me?'

but i shake my head,

'yes you do' she says,

and i get left there,

but an old man bending over the washbasin in the corner turns the tap on! and this is the end of me, i cant hold it in!

the warm wet patch is colding already when some sort of machine gets wheeled up on a trolley thing and two nurses are suddenly beside my bed talking,

'nngg' i try to explain,

but they put their hands on my shoulders and get hold of me and push me down and someone grips my legs too, so im trapped, and when i fight they lean on me and i struggle like hell and twist about, but the doctor smacks a mask over my face and the mask is covering my mouth as well as my nose, and he clamps it on to stop me wriggling free, but i cant breathe! and the room goes round like—

—got to get home,
—going to be *sick*!
—arms like dead lumps,
—cant seem to touch anything and fingers dont work,
—its like i dont *have* any arms,

so somethings been done to me, but all i know is that im crying already and the nurses push their smiling faces right up close to mine,

and i want to be tall, but its no good,

Gran says 'you *will* be'

and i hope so, especially now its my birthday and Uncle Ralph sent me an autograph book with different coloured pages and hes written in it and Mum sits right down to do a parrot painting for me on the next page, and i didnt even know she could *paint*!

'there!' she says 'make sure you leave it open to dry'

and i promise,

'tell him about our surprise' Mike says to her,

'what surprise?' i say,

and it doesnt look good,

'well' Mum says to me 'we all banded together to buy you something nice'

'for two weeks i put my pocket money in!' Di says,

and there it is on the kitchen table, a lonely parcel,

and already its begun ruining my day forever because its only one thing and of course i expect a different present from everyone the way they always get given,

'open it up' says Diana like shes more interested than i am,

and Michael gives the parcel a pat,

but ive been waiting and waiting to be eight, and now the day is here at last its all gone wrong,

Di tells Mum 'hes crying'

'am not!' i yell,

and i rip the string off because i hate this present already and its probably only a jigsaw puzzle with a thousand stupid pieces, so i rip the wrapping paper off,

'oh!'

and i never even dreamt about this,

a chemistry set glitters in there with little pots of powders and crystals and packs of things and an oil burner and test tubes, and each with its own place in the box where it belongs and looks beautiful,

'theres so much i want for you in life, darling' Mum says 'but most of all i want you to be happy'

'as long as he doesnt blow us all up!' Mike warns her,

but theres so many things i need to ask *you*,

hanging down from the gutter is the biggest icicle you ever saw because its thick like a tree trunk and all shiny and seems to come *up* from the yard so we go out and try hugging it but i cant reach the whole way round and my woollen gloves begin to stick,

and i love to visit Great-Uncle Monts tobacco shop in his little town, catching the bus out through the fields and over the hills because his shop is full of good smelling stuff that old men and young men buy or else soldiers but never ladies, and Great-Uncle Mont is puffing away on his pipe and his lips are wet and hes happy to see me and his pipe waggles,

'let me see your hand' he says,

i show him and he takes hold of it in his shaky old fingers and he turns it over to get a proper look,

'good' he says 'what i look for in a boy is ink stains'

'why?' i ask,

'because it shows me he can write' says Great-Uncle Mont 'and writing is the most important thing of all'

'more important than football?'

'what use is football' he says 'when theres a war?'

so now he gives me a cardboard box,

'happy birthday' he says,

and inside theres a printing set when i get the

string untied,

'so every time you want to print something' he says 'you fit these letters into the slots, here dyou see, on this wooden block?'

and its going to be easy because the letters are made of pink rubber,

'but you have to make your words *back-to-front* so they come out the right way when you print them'

i look at it and try to understand,

but the telephone rings so Great-Uncle Mont goes over and he puts his hairy ear against it,

'hullo?' he says into the box on the wall 'hullo?'

and he catches my eye,

'alright' he says to the telephone,

'its for you' he says to me,

but thats impossible,

'how?' i say,

'come on, son, round here behind the counter' he tells me,

and i dont know what to think,

'hop up on the stool' says Great-Uncle Mont 'and take hold of this thing'

and its warm when i put it against my ear,

'are you there, darling?' says Mums voice,

'yes' i say,

'no' says Great-Uncle Mont 'you have to talk into this part here' 'yes' i say again,

'im ringing to see that you got off the bus alright' Mum says,

and i can hear what she says though i cant hear *me*,

'are you at the office?' i say,

'yes'

'have you got a headache?'

'its not too bad, thank you' Mum says 'now pass the telephone back to Uncle Mont'

and all of a sudden i feel grown up,

'so now' i say to Great-Uncle Mont 'can i work the till?'

ive made my first word for printing and its a secret until i print it,

'i cant wait darling' Mum says because shes watching,

so i squish the block on the ink pad and then get the word square with the paper and now i print it,

RAPLH

and i have red ink stains all over my fingers,

'be careful not to smudge the page' Mike says,

and Mum reads the word ive made 'thats so sweet' she says,

and Mike looks at what ive done 'but look at it!' he says and begins cackling, so i do, but i cant see anything wrong,

'Ralph is a hard word to spell the right way round' she says 'let alone back to front'

and she brings me a new envelope from the drawer and tells me to print it again right in the middle and make it nice and clear, and nice and red,

'so i can send it to him in the post' she says.

8

So im like Rudolf Valentino in The Sheik and im going to ride horses and say 'do you know who i am?' and 'i am not accustomed to having my orders disobeyed' and there will be palm trees and brigands and robes and i shall say to the girl when i capture her 'you are so pretty, if i choose i can *make* you love me' and when i say this i know that its time to smile like him.

Mums sitting at the kitchen table having a cup of tea and a smoke and i kiss her on my way through but she catches hold of me and this is not a hug,

'just *look* at your neck!' she says,

and i squirm away but she catches me again and she means business,

'your ears! disgusting! and *behind* your ears! here!'

she tugs my shirt out from under my belt and pulls it up over my head, 'oh my goodness!' she says 'Michael, how did you let this child get so filthy!'

so Mike glares at me,

'im *cold*!' i tell her,

but Mum gets up and fetches the kettle off the stove and she pushes me into the bathroom, and people are always pushing me or pulling me, and she jams the plug in the washbasin plughole and mixes some cold water with the water from the kettle and starts *scrubbing* with a flannel,

'ow, ow that *hurts*!'

'its ingrained thats why' she says 'dont you ever wash? ever? now hold still'

'ow, ow!'

'and you can get busy with the towel when ive finished'

and she throws the flannel into the washbasin,

'and now look at that!' says Mum,

and shes turning her heel to look over her shoulder at the back of her leg because theres a ladder in her stocking as if thats my fault too, and i know about stockings because they are what Mum calls her cross, and i already know these ladders cost a lot because she likes to look nice all the time,

Gran cooked lamb shanks and they were delicious and im just mopping up my gravy with some bread, though

Joan just toys with hers, but what amazes me is Ken, and Ken is Joans fiancé who we are only just getting used to, because he picks up the bones and *sucks* them,

'the marrows the best part' Ken says and his mouth is shiny red and his face is red and his teeth are shiny and his moustache is black and his eyebrows are black 'a gentleman can suck marrowbone' Ken tells me,

so i give mine a try but the bone is slippery and when i get my lips around it i cant help slurping,

'whats it like in the artillery?' Mike says,

'the Royal Artillery Regiment' Ken tells us between sucks 'is the cream of the cream' and one by one he drops chunks of empty bone on his plate,

and i always know where i am with Gran because she talks such a lot, so when shes sitting at home she will say 'im about to get up' or 'i shall shell the peas directly' or she might say 'no one can tell me a single thing about rheumatism' or she might suddenly call out 'i dare say i should take a couple of Rennies for this indigestion' or just when you think shes dozed off in her chair she will say 'i ought stir my bones' and im not going to tell her it should be 'ought *to*' because she may not give me the threepence shes promised, and anyway she puts her hand flat on her tummy and asks me 'is this the heartburn or a touch of wind?' but she answers herself 'im sure i dont know' then she says to the ceiling 'i dont suppose youll fetch me my walking stick?' and when its put in her hand by magic she says 'oh what a little darlin you are!' and she tweaks my cheek and i call to Di and out we go,

our skittles are painted with red and yellow stripes but theyre mostly chipped and we set them up between the two skylights because the good thing about our yard is that its *flat* and the skylight is something the balls can roll up against and stop and the balls are yellow and theyre chipped too because we got given them for Christmas by Guy a long time ago before he went away,

and im the one whos been sent up here to the Red Cross shop because Mike thinks he spotted a valuable stamp and he rushed home to look it up in the Stanley Gibbons catalogue, but of course he cant just turn round and go back and buy it *now* or the shop ladys going to guess she put the wrong price on it, so thats why im here and i know what im to look for because its a yellow Baden-Baden unperforated ten pfennig stamp and ive remembered all this and Mike says i shall find it near the back of the big brown Red Cross album, and here it is right in front of my eyes, so i ask for some tweezers but the shop lady takes it out herself and pops it in a tiny envelope and sells it to me,

and Mikes down the road grinning and i grin back at him because we just bought the Baden-Baden stamp for twopence! and in Stanley Gibbons its worth a hundred and twelve POUNDS! so weve got to get home before someone catches us and takes it off us,

and back at home Diana gets out the magnifying glass for a good close look,

'its *mint*' she says 'its definitely mint'

'what?' says Mike,

'its mint' she says,

'i know that' i tell them,

'so its worth nothing!' Mike says,

and this is a dreadful shock and i cant believe hes telling the truth,

'but you *told* me to get it' i yell at him 'and i paid twopence for it'

'and twopence is exactly what its worth' Mike says,

'but you said!' i shout at him 'you said it was worth a hundred and twelve *pounds*!'

'because i thought it was *used*' Mike says 'and i was wrong'

so i knock the catalogue off the table and on to the floor,

'temper temper!' Di says,

but im not giving in and im never going to give in because a hundred and twelve pounds is enough to buy a *car* and 'used' only means its got a post office mark on it, so what about my printing set? because sometimes the post office mark is just a bit of a smudge on one corner and that counts just the same, and as for the glue i could just lick it off the back,

i press my nose up against the mirror in case im still like my father and his brother Ted but my face squashes and gets misty while i try to find things in my eyes when all there is is eyes and eyebrows and a flat nose, so i bare my teeth to look fierce instead but thats just silly and id laugh if i was in the mood, but even then i see something i dont want to see, so i wipe the mirror with my sleeve,

and when Mike stops outside Mr Norths shop we stop too and im looking in at the glass bottles in the window with their enormous round bottoms that are big enough for me to curl up inside, but theyve got long thin necks that nobody could get out through and glass stoppers,

'oy!' growls this tough voice behind us,

and its a bunch of kids watching and they walk our

way with jackets slung across their shoulders like capes and this is dangerous, and the twins are with them too and i recognise those prickly clothes and a jumper with the holes in it,

'oy!'

but i dont like the look of this because they block our way and even with Mike we will have no chance against so many if it comes to a fight and the twins dont like us ever since their mum thought we were their friends,

'dont say a word' Mike whispers 'leave it to me'

and he takes something out of his pocket,

and now i can see its one of our inventions! and i know all about it because i helped him make this, screwing two bolts into the same nut with some sulphur and stuff packed in there,

'look out!' Mike yells,

and he chucks it right at them,

but they dodge and it hits the wall and goes off BANG! and even im afraid though i was supposed to know,

and they back away and put their fists up and Mike gets all excited,

'want another?' he says and gets ready to chuck another at them,

but one of thems got an old watch that he looks at though i bet it doesnt work,

'just look at the time, Lord Muck!' he says 'youll be

late for your bath!' and they horse around and march off swinging their arms,

and i try picking the bolt up, but its too hot to touch,

school is a waste of time and im *fed up* with lessons and i never want to go back there and i get stitch in my side from running because im late and its impossible in every way that Mum can buy me a bike and *youre* not here to help, though i dont stop wanting one,

i cant get this tune out of my head that i end up whistling all the time and i whistle my way from the kitchen into the lounge room,

'for Petes sake put a sock in it!' Mike yells at me,

and i can hear a voice down in the street calling 'hullo there!'

and its a man but Dianas the one who gets up to see,

'hey!' the voice calls 'are those Hall scalliwags at home?'

'is it for *us*?' i say,

anyhow Mike rushes to the window now and so do i because i dont want to miss anything,

'Uncle Ralph!' Mike shouts,

and i look down but theres only a stranger there shading his eyes against the sun and its nobody i know,

'is that really Uncle Ralph?' Di whispers,

but it cant be because i dont remember *him*,

Mike calls out 'whose car?'

'what car?' the stranger says,

but theres a sports car parked right beside him,

so i yell '*there!*' and point,

and he jumps away from it like someone getting an electric shock,

'what? not again! officer, arrest this car! its following me!'

i laugh because thats so ridiculous!

'what do you think, Titch?' the stranger calls to me 'should i catch it out?' and he puts a finger to his lips while he tiptoes around it,

'yes!' Diana screams,

but i yell 'no! you silly!'

and the stranger leans in and grabs hold of the wheel and the horn toots,

'it doesnt like that!' he says 'but ive got it by the neck so its safe for you to come down now'

'is he the real Uncle Ralph?' i ask Mike,

but the stranger down there says 'come and find out' and he lights a cigarette,

i hide below the sill but i can smell his tobacco,

'can two squeeze into the back?' Mike asks 'if ones in the front?'

'how many escaped prisoners do you have then?'

'three' Diana calls down,

and i spring up again so he can see for himself,

'thats just enough and not too many' he says,

but Mike says 'does Mum even know youre here?'

and i bet she doesnt, i just *bet* she doesnt,

so i yell out for her 'Mum, Mum!'

and without waiting for an answer i race around the flat until i find her in the yard pegging out some washing,

and so i tell her 'he says—, he says—' but then i hear doors start slamming away inside the flat 'he says—'

Mike charges past behind my back singing out 'its Uncle Ralph downstairs'

and already Mums untying her apron and she smiles,

'lets see what the fuss is about' she says and takes my hand,

but the others have already reached the corner at the end of the lane, out of the shadows and into the sunny street where they dance around the stranger who lifts Di up and sticks a big kiss on her cheek,

'i bags' she says talking right into his face 'i bags the front seat'

'Ralph!' cries Mum,

so it *is* him,

and the stranger kisses her too,

'poor old Dods, you look tired' he says 'now then you lot, stand at ease and heres the drill, there are rules for kids in cars, beginning with rule number twenty-three-and-a-half, and rule twenty-three-and-a-half states that each time we stop you have to switch seats so you all get a turn in the front'

'hullo' says Uncle Ralph to me 'is this the serious one?'

he shakes my hand and there are sandy hairs on his wrist,

and its the *thickest warmest* hand ever,

so i grin at him because now hes my uncle and he twitches his nose like a rabbit and starts whispering in my ear 'theres talk on the network that your tongue got slashed by the enemy'

'i came a proper cropper!'

everyones crowding round him,

'a proper cropper?' he laughs 'give us a look at it, Titch'

so i stick my tongue right out for him to see, and Uncle Ralph is the only man in the world who ever called me Titch and he takes his time and then he shakes his head 'thats a champion tongue so i suppose it must have taken seventy-seven stitches to fix?'

'five' Mum says,

but i was going to tell him eight,

'you could have fooled me' he puts on some sun-glasses to squint at it again,

'it hurt like hell' i tell him,

'i bet it did'

and Mum tut-tuts,

'now then kids, when i say go you can all hop into my

car' Uncle Ralph says,

and he holds up his hand like a policeman to stop us moving and we wait and we wait,

'*Go*!'

Mikes first and even though theres no proper seat in the back he climbs in just the same and perches on the ledge there,

'thats right' Uncle Ralph tells him,

and im beside Mike and Dis in the front and Mum waves and we wave back,

and we are off already and wind dashes my hair about faster and faster and the shops move away behind us getting smaller and smaller, and we zoom around corners and suddenly huge gasometers swing at me and i duck,

'whats that pedal on the left?' Mike asks and points down past Uncle Ralphs shoulder,

'thats the clutch' Uncle Ralph says,

'whats the clutch?' i ask,

'a thing that gets the gears going'

'whats the gears?' i ask,

'the gears make the car go' Uncle Ralph says,

and up we swoop over the top of a hill and down into a dip so my tummy drops and i have to hang on like mad,

but Michael shouts 'whoo-oops!'

and we get the idea,

so at the next dip we shout 'whoo-oops!'

but the car slows down and stops and Uncle Ralph

pulls the handbrake on,

'heres a stroke of luck' he says pointing across a field 'do you see what those women are doing?'

and the army women wear uniforms,

'whats *that*?' says Di 'what are they standing round?'

'a barrage balloon' Mike says 'half full of gas'

but already its big like an elephant and all slumpy the way it lolls on the ground,

'look!' i say,

because the tail fins fill and pop up and the whole huge thing rolls and straightens and the cables all around stretch tight, and it starts lifting off the ground,

'this is fantastic' Mike says,

and the women get hold of some ropes and dole them out hand-over-hand so that the balloon only gets to rise a bit at a time,

'shall we put our money on the WAAFs' Uncle Ralph asks and he pats my head with his big warm hand 'or the Loch Ness monster?'

'the Loch Ness monster is a *snake*' i tell him,

'is that a fact?' he says 'well, i never!'

and the WAAFs have trouble keeping their feet on the ground but theyre like a tug-of-war team,

'see how determined they are' Uncle Ralph says 'hanging on like that'

and the balloon already looks as if its stuck halfway up in the sky,

Uncle Ralph gets out to stretch his legs and he starts us cheering so we jump about and wave our arms, but the women dont bother about us or anything,

'dare you to start it!' i say to Mike when he jumps into the drivers seat and tinkers with the knobs,

'this is the fuel gauge' he shows me and taps it and he knows the names of everything already 'and this is the dashometer'

'perhaps id better drive' says Uncle Ralph 'i begin to suspect you might be that young Michael Hall, the famous daredevil'

and so Mike slips over to the passenger side and Di gets in beside me and we watch Uncle Ralph drive with the gearstick and i reckon i could do that because it doesnt look hard, and we race right up to the crossroads where we slow down,

'which way now?' says Uncle Ralph,

and i yell 'left!'

so thats the way we go,

'why *dont* you come home more often?' Di says 'we want to see you'

and i get a bright idea and i say 'so does Olive'

but Mike reaches back to hit me over the head,

'ah' Uncle Ralph mutters 'Olive'

and he steers the car,

and Mike says 'these are hairpin bends!'

and we zoom under an arch of leaves with shadows

flickering all over the bonnet and all over everyones hair,

'*Popeyes* sweetheart is called Olive' i say,

and i get a good look at Uncle Ralph's cheeks that are so red he must scrub them too hard, and i wonder if all he ever does is wash his face and shave his chin and drive his car around in the wind, and i cant wait for us to stop again because this time itll be my turn to sit in the front,

'dont worry' Uncle Ralph says as if he knows what im thinking 'young Michael will obey the rules'

and soon the time comes for me to get settled,

'ready, sir?' says Uncle Ralph,

and i can only nod because i cant make any words come,

'stand by' says Uncle Ralph, saluting, and then the engine *rawls* and hills and fields begin to fly away behind us, and i have to lift my bottom to save it getting scraped because the bitumen is skimming so *close* underneath me,

and we could go on like this forever and ever because the best thing in the whole world is a car, and the best thing in a car is sitting next to the driver, but the worst thing is seeing our town come up ahead with the same old houses and telegraph wires, and having to slow down for the same old people to cross at the same old Belisha beacon and then stopping altogether outside the same old bakery opposite Lewises, still, its pretty good sitting in the car and i dont care if showing off is bad because everybody notices, but Michaels busy taking a close look at the dials,

'we drove eighteen miles' he says,

and my lucky number is eighteen because thats when my birthday is, and he gives me his big sunglasses to try on,

'yum yum' says Uncle Ralph pointing to a dish of cream buns in the shop window 'hop to it, Mike, and buy us four of the squashiest' he says 'heres a shilling'

'yum yum!' we say all together in a chorus,

so Michael darts off to join the queue at the counter,

'once upon a time' Uncle Ralph tells Diana and me 'your mother had her shop just up the road here'

'and what happened next?' i say,

'she sold baby clothes and things' he says 'but the other shopkeepers in this forgotten backwater drove her out of business because they said she had got too posh for them and the poor old dear, so it would seem, never got over it'

but i dont remember a shop and anyway i feel important because theres a lady staring at us and she just came out of Lewises where they have frocks in the window and she looks like a rich person from London because she frowns and digs around in her purse so i suddenly get a terrible idea and nudge Diana,

'help!' i whisper,

because what i reckon is that this must be Uncle

Ralphs *wife* coming over to catch him out and take him off us, and she crosses the road and shes wearing a veil with little dots and Uncle Ralph looks up,

'good afternoon' he says,

but she doesnt say anything back, so she cant be his wife after all, *whew!* because wives always have to answer, but shes going to give him something,

'what is it?' i whisper,

'just a feather' Di whispers back,

yes, its a little old feather that she must have got off a white duck by the look of it, and a bit crumpled too,

but Uncle Ralph says nothing,

and all through the body of the car i can feel the motor running,

so the lady whos not his wife waits for him to take the feather off her and it shivers in the wind, and at last he tucks it away in his inside pocket,

but Di speaks up and says to her 'we dont know *you*!'

and because Uncle Ralph is quiet i say 'we dont like you'

'children!' he warns us,

but the lady just stands and stares while her ears go red around her earrings and she clips her purse shut with gold knobs like ball-bearings and her nails are painted bright red, and i hate her because this is Gomorrah and shes a bitch and a *tart* and i bet she goes into telephone booths!

and even the butchers boy watches her rush away from us and back up the steps into Lewises, and hes still pedalling along on his bicycle and he only just misses a lorry knocking him over because he swerves just in time!

'well i never!' Uncle Ralph says at last,

but his voice is really soft,

'now *that*' says Uncle Ralph 'was unexpected'

and the little bell above the bakers door tinkles when Mike comes out,

'you missed it' i tell him,

'what?' Mike says,

'nothing' says Uncle Ralph,

'but—' says Di,

'*nothing*' says Uncle Ralph,

and who cares? now Mikes doling out cream buns and i take my first mouthful and its a big creamy bite,

and Uncle Ralph says 'thanks Michael' though he pops his own back in the paper bag and tucks it away under the seat,

Mums got a new song,

'let the bright seraphim in burn-ing row' she sings 'their bright up-lift-ed angel trum-pets blow'

and her voice is so loud and so high i throw myself back against the wall as if shes knocked me out, 'let the cher-u-bic hosts—' she sings,

and im flopping and twitching all over the place and shes laughing so much she cant sing anymore,

and my idea is to go to Mrs Harrises hotel to say hullo,

'but she wont want us in there without Mike' Di says,

'yes she will' i say 'if we offer to help'

'what with?'

'anything'

'like washing?' Di suggests,

and the corridor is gloomy and the lino is brown, but suddenly the bar door crashes open and these soldiers stagger through,

'watch out!' Di shrieks,

so i dodge down towards the kitchen, but the soldiers come that way too and theyre arguing and shoving and there are four of them and they look pretty rough so they cant be Americans, and i get squashed against the wall,

'Rod!' Di yells,

but im right here at the open door,

'ya bloody mug!' one soldiers shouting,

and i watch them cross the yard and stamp around in the rain, splashing in puddles and bumping up against the old water butt thats got green slime on it, and they shout right in each others faces, 'im gonna get ya for that!'

'you and who else?'

'ya mug!'

and first the punch makes a smacking sound on his jaw but he starts laughing, and now theyre all laughing and hanging around and everythings alright,

'Rod!' says Di,

and shes waiting for me at the front door,

home from school i keep scratching because my head itches and Dianas the same so Mum gets a close look,

'youve caught nits!' she says 'how disgusting!'

and she washes her hands and she doesnt love us anymore because we are dirty,

'the nits are the eggs' Mike explains to us 'and we have to get rid of them before they can hatch out into little crawly things that swarm all over your head, so thats what this special comb is for because its a metal comb and the teeth are really really close together'

and i can see that only the hair can get through, but the comb does just a few at a time,

'are these little bud things the eggs?' Di asks Mike while shes doing me,

and he only nods because hes reading, but they dont look like what i call eggs,

and i make a cradle with my hands so i can hold one of the big floppy red flowers growing outside Grans new house in Lansdowne Crescent,

'whats this called, Gran?'

'thats a peony bush' she says,

'is the flower a peony too?'

'yes of course' Mum says,

and i like it,

'but why have you moved, Granny?' Di asks,

'and what happened to New Mills Court?' i ask,

but Gran looks bothered 'i sold it, darlin'

Di asks 'did you get a lot of money?'

'youll understand when you grow up' Gran says,

and thats what i hate being told but shes got rheumatism so bad because she has to rock from side to side when she walks,

'this house is too poky' i tell her,

and Mum frowns and says 'Joan will be here in a minute' and she shakes her head at me 'bringing a thermos and some biscuits'

'i think i shall take another look upstairs' Gran says and she sets off gasping and slow,

the stairs creak and Gran stops halfway 'i suppose it is a bit poky' she says to me 'and thats why i had to put most of my furniture in store'

so we tramp up after her,

'such a how dyou do!' Gran explains 'the wardrobes

were too big to get through the front door!'

'but youll feel better, dear' Mum says 'when the carpets are down'

'everythings dusty' i say,

'well this house' says Gran 'is what i can afford now'

and i unlatch a bedroom window so i can lean out over the little front garden and spit on the peonies,

'who bought your nice old house, Gran?' Di asks,

'Olive Freestones mother'

'but theyve got their own!' Di says,

'*and* with a bead curtain too' i say,

but i cant even hang around with Di today because shes the flower girl and im nothing, so she has to stand beside Joan and Joans in her white wedding dress and Kens in his Artillery uniform and theyre up on top of the church steps being photographed and the organs still going inside, and im sick of weddings so i go and kick an old can around among the graves in the churchyard and theres some kids from school watching the photographer move his camera on legs but i dont know their names, and Great-Uncle Mont sits on a bench smoking in a quiet corner while his pipe jumps up and down on his bottom lip and his tobacco smells better than anyones,

'come over here and talk to me' he says in his deep

shaky voice 'so what do you think of your little aunty getting married?'

'she looks like a ghost' i say,

he takes out the wet stem to have a chuckle and his big old teeth are yellow and crooked,

'im bored' i tell him,

'thats because youre full of too much life'

and even his knees shake so much he has to hold on to them with his big hands,

'you look nice' i tell him because hes wearing a grey hat,

and he raises it when some ladies pass by along the footpath,

'whats new?' Great-Uncle Mont says to me,

and i dont know how to tell him what they said on the BBC news because we arent allowed to talk about any old war on account of his memories and how he got hurt a long time ago,

'so are we beating Hitler?' he rumbles,

'no' i say 'Hitlers going to win'

'ahhh!' he says and shakes his head 'well that would be a tragic day'

'would it?' i say,

'the Naziss are more terrible than anyone' he says 'so you can take it from me that if we ever give in we are goners'

and i look at the hairs sprouting from his ears and

from his nose and its as if his whole heads full of hairs trying to get out,

'then we wont' i say,

and he turns to look at me and his eyes are sad with pink saggy skin around them, and suddenly i know i am going to tell him my secret that ive never told anyone before,

'when we win the war' i say 'im going to run away' i say 'to Kangaroo Valley'

and Great-Uncle Mont pats my shoulder,

'take a look at the happy couple' he says and he tilts his shaky head,

at the top of the church steps the photographer photographs Ken standing at attention with three captains pips on his shoulders and Joan holding on to his arm,

'thank you' the photographer says though they didnt do anything,

and now they can move they smile and come down into a whole snowstorm of confetti flying about in the air,

'when you have the chance to be happy' Great-Uncle Mont tells me 'take hold of it'

but here comes Pam walking along the street with her big sister so i run across to surprise them,

'its my auntys wedding' i say,

'is she having a baby?' Pams sister asks,

'i dont think so'

and they keep walking because theyre in a hurry,
Pam says 'so long' just like me,
'so long' i say because shes my pal,

and Mr Marks gets straight to business about the war because he knows everything and the great thing is that new battles keep happening so hes always got something more to tell,

'the only good thing about this disastrous conflict' he says 'is that if you little Philistines pay attention it may teach you geography'

and Philistines is how he starts just about every lesson,

'Germany is here to our east' he teaches us 'so which way do their bombers have to fly if they wish to drop their bombs on us?'

'west' says Pam,

'west indeed' he says and he goes on 'there are U-boats in the Skagerrak, right? they are on their way to the River Severn, right? you, boy, come up here to the map of Europe and show the class where the Skagerrak is and where the Severn is and which direction the U-boat must take'

and Mr Marks lets me sharpen Pams pencil as well as my own and i do it because i like working the machine thats fixed to the teachers table, and when you stick the pencil in at one end and turn the handle you can smell the wood being cut, but im careful not to keep the pencil in there too long because then the lead breaks off and its a waste and you have to begin all over again,

but Mum says Pam has a hard face, though it looks soft to me and it *is* soft when i touch it with my finger, so i write Pam a letter signed SWALK anyway,

and there are lots of old holes in my desk that other kids have dug with penknives for me to fill with ink,

i want you to speak to me but then i *dont* want you to speak to me and im never going to ask ever again because i dont care!

and the library book Mum brings home is called The White Feather so i remember something and i tell her about that lady giving Uncle Ralph the white feather the day he took us out in the car, and she bursts into tears,

and Mike twists my arm behind my back,

'they only give white feathers to cowards' he hisses in my ear, well *he* didnt see and i did and i saw that tart and her nail polish and her high heels, but even so i think she maybe meant to give it to me instead of Uncle Ralph, though im not going to tell anyone, and the only person in the world i still love is Olive,

and Joan,

and the hole in my pocket is big enough to get my hand through so i fiddle with myself and theres no one to smack my hand away because im out and Mums back at home,

we all run out across the playground and the girls whisper to their friends while we play tag and im good at this because im a fast runner and every time its my turn i keep tagging this one boy thats supposed to be a bully and hes never even said hullo before but im happy and i like him because hes famous, and here in the yard you can skim around and get dizzy because its all kids and no grown-ups, and im faster than him so he cant get away from me and i tag him again,

'you!' he shouts too close up to my face,

and he pushes me in the chest,

'hullo' i say,

and i give him my cheeky smile but what he does is to spit at me and i dont know why, so theres spit on my coat and maybe the best place to wipe it off is the school wall,

'you!' he yells 'ya *look* at me when i spit at ya!'

so i spit back,

and i see his fist coming but i cant move,

and my face gets punched and his fist is such a shock and so *hard*,

'smashing!' says somebody that i cant see,

and im hurt worse than ever before, except sometimes when i fall down, so i swing at him now hes my enemy, only i miss and my fist just goes through the air, and somehow he bobs back up and hits me again, and i take another swing but i still cant hit him,

'didnt your dad never teach ya nothin?' he yells,

and he hits me so many times i cant think, but i know im crying and when i touch my face i get blood on my fingers and so i keep trying to hit him back but he dodges away too fast every time,

and he punches my face again,

so i scream and suddenly i know this is what i must do,

i stand in the playground and scream and scream,

and Mikes telling us about what he remembers and i ask 'how did he die, Mike?'

'well' Mike says 'he waved goodbye from the hospital window'

and i think back to when i was little and i think about everything, but even when i squeeze my memory i dont see any man waving from a window, and i dont remember a face at all and the only things i can think of are useless,

'but *how* did he die?' i ask,

'i dont know' Michael says 'im not a doctor'

and just around the bend we come to the stone wall and the stile that we climb over, out of the sunshine and into the woods, and all around us the woods are lovely and dark and quiet and the air smells mouldy and soft and leaves brush against my chest,

'come on, you kids' Mike says with a grin because we love the woods 'lets head straight down to the stream this time' and so we do and theres water gurgling against the bank but still no way to get to the other side,

'i reckon im big enough to jump across' Mike says,

'then what about *us*?' says Di,

and i know Mike would rather hang around with other big boys doing things like jumping,

'go on' i dare him 'try'

and i want him to fall in,

but instead he finds some stepping stones and begins hopping down the stream from one stone to another, and i want to be just like him, but the stones wobble and the rushing water is brown like tea, and now Dis stuck on one thats big as a football so Mike jumps down beside her to help her balance but he misses and splashes in,

'nice try!' i say because thats what Ken says, so i know itll get him,

but he doesnt seem to care because hes up again and dancing around while Di follows,

and now im giddy from staring into the water,

'why dont we head over that way?' Di says now shes safe on the bank,

'good idea' Mike agrees 'up the slope and when we get to the top we shall be able to see where we are'

and i go up like a giant because of my handholds and footholds, all the time thinking about the woods and the animals and especially Ratty and Mole in The Wind in the Willows and we are surprised to discover some caves that go quite deep where i spy a dead beetle on a stone and its got a brown shell that glows green so i pick it up for our collection, and after we poke around in the caves enough we get to the top where we can charge down the other side while the ground crumbles under our shoes and its all muddy and skiddy with loose stones and stuff so i have to run or else i shall topple head over heels,

'do you think Uncle Ralph will ever come again?' i say,

but Mike doesnt bother answering, he just breaks off a branch and swings it to cut a path through the weeds, so i give him my beetle to keep and he takes it and cups it in his hand and tilts his head on one side to get a better look and then he puts it in his shirt pocket and he ruffles my hair,

but ive noticed something new and its an awful thing because theres this hornet hovering right in front of my face,

'watch out, dreamy!' Di shrieks 'watch out!'

i dont know what to do,

'keep calm, Rod' Mike says,

'kill it!' i beg, because the hornet is going to sting me,

but they just stand back and watch,

'its too fast to hit' Mike says and swings his stick at something else,

'if you stay still' Di tells me 'maybe it wont notice you'

but it *has* noticed me and thats why it swivels on the spot, 'kill it!' i say,

and my knees are bare and my arms as well!

but they both back off,

'you *beasts*!' i yell at them,

but Mike keeps walking on through a patch of ferns and Di follows him lifting her arms like shes wading in a pool of water up to her chest, so i growl at the hornet and show it my teeth 'grrr!' i growl, and suddenly i dont see it anymore so that worked and it must have flown off, and now i suppose i shall have to follow the others but first i break off a stick of my own and whip a whole patch of thistles till the stems are broken and the heads flop,

'when it comes back' i say, running to catch up 'i hope it chases you'

but Mike just keeps on making a track for us,

'there was nothing we could do' he tells me,

'so where are we going?' Di whines,

'this way' he says and puts his hand on her back to push her along in front of him,

'this is an awful walk' Di says,

'it could be worse' Mike says,

'it could be raining' i say,

'i reckon youve got us lost' she says,

Mike groans like he does,

'oh, you two!'

and Di digs her heels in because she wont move a

single step further, not even when he gives her another good shove,

'come on, Rod' he says to me,

and he grabs hold of my shirt and we leave her behind while im thinking about how to get revenge on them both, thats what the woods are like with no one able to hear or see us and me busy thinking while i walk,

Mike says 'i like the name Boris'

but im worried about Diana so i turn round to see how shes going and shes plodding along behind with her head down and her plaits bobbing, and her ears are pink but i cant see her face so i dont know if shes okay or not, and the truth is that we are probably lost,

'ssh!' Mike says suddenly,

and he stops and hes listening, but theres nothing to listen to, so i just swish my stick,

'*ssh!*' he says,

and Diana hurries to catch us up,

'where are we?' she says,

'i think i can hear something' says Mike,

'im cold' i complain,

'good thing we brought our jumpers' Mike says,

but mine is really a girls cardigan because it was once Dianas and im too embarrassed to put it on at school where the kids would kill me, though now we are lost theres no one to see so i dig it out and stick my arms into the arm holes, ‘you look stupid’ Mike says and grins at me,

‘i dont care’ i tell him because i shall take it off once we are out of the woods,

‘this is just the place for snakes’ he says,

and i dont care about snakes either so i hang back just to annoy him and Di hangs back too and shes dawdling with me so we start dawdling together and our legs are all scratched and bloody,

‘i hate Mike’ she says,

and she *tramps* along beside me,

‘i hate him too’ i tell her,

and we start kicking the grass flat,

‘look up there!’ Mike shouts,

‘what is it?’ Di asks,

‘a fence!’ he says, pointing,

and sure enough hes right, so this must mean we are trespassing,

‘barbed wire’ Mike warns us ‘watch out for the rust because one scratch and youll catch Lock Jaw off it’

‘how?’ says Di,

‘Lock Jaw means you cant eat or drink’ Mike tell us ‘so a nurse has to feed you through a tube’

‘can you *talk*?’ i ask,

‘i dont think so’ Mike says ‘anyway you die if you catch it’

but the thing about this wire is the dead animals strung up on it, ‘ugh!’ says Diana and spits and pinches her nose,

so i spit too,

‘this ones a fox’ Mike says,

and i think of Grans fox fur that she wears round her neck because that fox is dead too, but this one is all mangy and dry and flat like a lump of rubber, and we see a dead bat there and a squirrel stretched out on the wire and tied up by its little paws with its tail hanging down,

‘crucified’ Mike whispers and takes out his notepad because hes going to be a policeman when he grows up or a vet and he begins drawing but im scared now so i look around in case the kids who did this are watching us,

im being careful not to let the fence scratch me

‘who could kill a *squirrel*!’ Di wails ‘thats so sad’ and she starts to cry,

‘these animals must have been caught and strung up as a warning to others’ Mike says,

and hes all eyes and ears like me, but suddenly he drops down among the ferns so his head is the only thing sticking up,

‘ssh!’

we duck down too and he puts a finger on his lips then points among the stems,

‘have a look over that way but be quick about it’ he says ‘in case youre seen’

and i pop up but theres nothing and i get scared so i duck back down again,

Di takes a turn,

'grown-ups!' she whispers 'all in a circle'

then i have a second go and shes right, there are *people* sitting in among the tree trunks,

'gypsies' Mike says,

'lets clear out before they catch us' Di whispers,

and Mike begins creeping away among the ferns and i take extra care to lift my feet when i copy him but the ferns rustle and twigs snap,

'quiet!' he hisses at me 'or youll get us killed!'

im *being* as quiet as i can and its not my fault when i trip over,

'OW!'

and the pains awful and im on the ground and theres a gash across my leg, but i dont dare cry,

Di looks and she covers her mouth,

'oh!' she says,

but its not my leg shes looking at,

'ooh-er!' she says,

and now i see that what tripped me was a sagging strand of barbed wire,

'Mike!' i say 'help!'

and he hoists my arm across his shoulders to help me up and we find the path and thats the way we go,

'i can feel the Lock Jaw' i say,

'the point is' he tells me 'to get you safely to the road'

and once we are out of the woods i sit on the stile

with my cardigan wrapped tight around me and this is the worst thing ever in all my life because the rusty wire got me and im going to die now, but Mikes talking to a farmer and the farmer sits high up on his tractor and Mike points my way so i keep mopping the blood with my handkerchief, and the farmer shakes his head but at last he climbs down to come over,

'give us a look, sonny' he says,

and his breath smells bad but hes careful the way he holds my leg in his fingers and he turns the wound this way and that to get a proper look at it,

'nobbut a scratch' he says,

'it doesnt hurt' i lie,

'what about the Lock Jaw?' Di says,

'Lock Jaw!' the man says and gets his own jaw working 'can you feel it, then?' he asks me,

'i think so' i say,

and now its too late to stop my tears coming, because this is the end and because hes seen me in a girls cardigan too,

'who told you about Lock Jaw?' he says and he takes hold of my chin so he can try wiggling that too,

'Michael did' says Di,

'no no' he tells Mike 'it feels loose as can be, and as for that cut there, well tis a good open cut'

'thank you' says Mike,

but its *me* thats going to die!

'tell him to keep his leg moving' says the farmer as if im not here anymore 'and so long as it can bleed the little chap has nowt to fear' and he pats *Mike* on the back and goes back over to his tractor,

'we saw some gypsies in the woods' Di tells him,

'well then' he says 'when they come around selling clothes pegs to your mum youll know where they live, wont you?

and he climbs on, and the little lid on his tractor chimney bats up, letting out a puff of smoke when the big tyres begin to turn,

we hang round just outside the gate at New Mills Court now it doesn't belong to Gran just to get a look at Olives dreadful mother while shes digging in the garden with a trowel and ripping out the plants,

'those are Grans pansies' i tell her through the bars of the gate,

'dont tell me!' she shouts 'and whens your Uncle Ralph ever going to get that divorce of his? when? just you answer me that, because im all ears waiting to hear' and she stabs at the ground 'he said he wouldnt ever go back to that woman and her children in Australia, but just you wait and see'

'its not our fault' i say,

'he doesnt keep his word to *anybody*' she says 'your Uncle Ralph'

and Grans nice old house has changed because the curtains are closed in the middle of the day,

'and my Olive forty already!' Mrs Freestone says,

and she gets busy digging again and her wild grey hair stands out all over the place,

'then *i* shall marry her' i say,

and i show her my Valentino eyes,

and i know that you were in a hospital too, but if you never had stitches in your tongue you wont have any *idea* how much they get in the way or how much they hurt, specially if they were put in crooked like mine,

the best way of getting into the cinema free is to hang around outside during the interval, but this is the first time i ever tried it alone,

and here come the people with their Pass Outs,

'do you want that ticket?' i ask a lady carrying a cat in her shopping basket,

'this?' she says and holds up the Pass Out,

but i only nod because now im embarrassed,

'clear off!' she says 'you little pest!'

and now its old Mrs North and shes the chemists wife so she knows me and because she might tell Mum and get me into trouble i dodge out of sight behind an usherette while the swing doors keep swinging, but i keep an eye on two ladies who stop on the pavement for a chat,

'shall we go to the tea rooms and have a bite of lunch?' says the one with a walking stick,

'theres no time' says the other,

and they tuck their Pass Outs in their purses while theyre looking around, so theyre no good,

but here comes my chance because a young woman reaches for the wall and leans against it looking really sick,

'excuse me' i say,

'thanks, but im alright' she tells me,

and shes holding her tummy in her hands and she smiles and i can see its because shes going to have a baby,

'are you sure?'

'yes'

'do you need your Pass?' i ask,

'oh you wouldnt want to see whats coming on next, love' she says and her face cramps up 'its a horror!'

ive heard about horror films that theyre very exciting and now i know what its going to be i really want to see it, but she shoves her Pass at one of the usherettes who takes it, hell! and im hopping mad because if i dont get in soon someones going to catch me,

'HHHRRRAFFF!' an old geezer coughs in my face and goes purple and his red eyes glare at me and he puts his Pass in my hand without a word, Wow! just wait till i tell the kids at school!

but the usherette says 'i didnt notice you coming out'

'i came through the other door'

'but you have to have an accompanying adult to see this film'

i never thought of that,

'my Aunty Olives in there waiting for me' i say,

she looks at the Pass as though it might be a fake,

'well all i can say' she says 'is that im surprised at her'

and my favourite thing at the cinema is watching the curtains, and im just waiting for whats going to happen because the lights always go dim and everyone can see the curtains are made of thick dark red stuff and i can never work out *how* they change into invisible material but thats what happens every time, so up pops J Arthur Rank and we can see him hitting a huge gong but we are watching him *through* the curtains, and now the curtains split apart and sure enough there he is on the screen behind, so this proves it and i reckon it may have something to do with the X-ray but i dont know for sure,

the big film is about some lady who gets murdered in a gloomy old house that belongs to a man with one leg, and hes stuck in a wheelchair so he cant be the one who did the murder because it happens upstairs, but the very next night someone else is for it when the murderers shoes go tramping and limping along the same passage with a heavy step, but in the morning the people all eat their breakfast in the garden sitting beside a pond where theres an island with a stone statue of a man with no clothes on, and theres a detective like Guy who spies on everybody till the police ask him what he has found out, and he says 'it baffles me' but hes the next one strangled and the mystery is that the wheelchair man is the only one who doesnt have an alibi, so the policemen dont know what to think, except for a young constable hiding in the bushes after dark and he watches the lights go on in the house and he cant believe his eyes! because one leg of the stone statue out in the lake begins to vanish and soon its gone altogether, and now the heavy feet go tramping through the house like one of thems made of stone so someone else is going to get it in the neck, but i cant see because ive got my hands over my eyes and im going to hide like this till its all over at the end,

i hate wearing braces to keep my shorts up, so thats why i have a belt and this belt is green and black with a buckle like an S and the S is really a snake and the snake is silver with scales and an eye and i love it,

'you little Philistines need to learn that you are not important' says Mr Marks 'because the rest of the world will get on quite nicely without any of you'

Pam sits beside me and we are both on best behaviour, and Mr Marks lines the whole class up alongside the Greenline coach we came in,

'today we are visiting a munitions factory' he says 'and this will help explain the war effort'

so we file indoors where its huge but theres nothing to see,

'the ladies here are drilling the metal' Mr Marks says,

and there are *hundreds* of them in overalls with scarves tied round their heads and their sleeves rolled up standing at work alongside lines of machines and theres a factory man with a beard whos showing us round and he points to a machine with some white stuff like milk streaming out of a nozzle,

'this is the *flux*' he says 'to cool the hot brass'

and though ive seen lots of beards in storybooks his is the first one ive seen in real life,

'understand?' Mr Marks snaps at us 'and why does metal get hot when its drilled?'

'friction, sir' says Trevor Tomkins the class pet,

'good boy'

'whats happening over there?' i ask the factory man because i want to see his beard move,

'those are the lathes, sonny' he says 'where we manufacture shell cases'

and the women *lathing* have to stand still while little heaps of brass shavings get all over their shoes,

'and through here' says the man with the beard 'the shell bodies are made, ready for fitting into the cases'

'is it dangerous?' Pam asks,

'no, sweetheart, we dont handle explosives in this outfit' he says '*our* product gets shipped out to Buckinghamshire for that'

several of the women working look up at us but they dont smile, and theres pliers and iron blocks and black oil and grease everywhere except on the shiny shells,

'can i touch?' i ask,

'no' says Mr Marks,

but at the same time the factory man says 'yes, if you like'

so i do and Mr Marks frowns at me,

'why are there twenty-eight?' i ask because ive counted the hollow shells that stand in crates like milk bottles,

'i dont answer silly questions' says the man,

and already we are being lined up ready to march

through to the next part for us to see what they are making in there,

'so when England wins the war' Mr Marks tells us in front of everyone 'its these ladies we shall have to thank'

and when he starts clapping we clap too, but it seems silly,

and one of the women wipes her nose with her forearm,

everythings changed because we find some strange kids sitting around on the grass beside our canal, just exactly in *our* spot and theyre scrambling to their feet and this means trouble,

so Diana faces them and plants her hands on her hips and i wish we had waited for Mike to come with us,

'thats where we sit' she tells them though its just her and me,

and the leader comes straight up to us looking pretty rough and he shoves her aside to get at me,

'ere!' he says 'whats your name?'

he shakes his fist in my face,

and im afraid of fists but ive got to pretend im not scared because Guy once told me that you can *smell* peoples fear and i think this boy may smell mine, ‘cat got your tongue?’ he says and shoves his face right up close so all i can think about was the day that bully punched me in the playground,

‘yep!’ i say,

but i dont dare move because i dont want him to get a whiff of my smell or anything,

‘little smarty-pants ay?’

but suddenly he staggers right up against me because Di butts him in the back,

‘hey!’ he yells at her,

and this means trouble when hes got hold of her arm and yanks her round,

‘leave her alone!’ i shout,

and hes holding on to her, but its like theyre pals already and hes grinning and so he puts out his hand to me,

‘dyou kids want to muck about with us, then?’ he says,

and nothing like this ever happened before,

‘not half!’ i say,

and its like his hand is a hard old glove the way it feels in mine,

‘the names Jack’ he says,

and Jacks our pal so we are never going to need Michael again,

‘Jacks tougher than anybody’ says one boy opening and shutting a penknife,

‘yeah? well, i bet my father could beat his father’ i say,

but Diana shoots me a shocked look,

'you a screw loose or summat?' Jack says and he cuffs the back of my head,

and a boy with both front teeth missing grins right in my face 'put a sock in it why dontya!' he says,

and the boy with the knife gets busy cutting cigarettes from an old-mans-beard bush so we can all smoke,

'woodbines' he says,

'even me *brother* could probly beat your father' Jack says to me 'es twelve and once e hit a full-grown man and kept hitn im' and Jack gets a bit of spit in the corner of his mouth 'ten or twenty times *smack smack smack,* like that, till e knocked im down!'

'i saw im too' one of the kids in the grass says,

'*and*' says the boy without teeth 'hedve beat him down again if hedve got up!'

'there e was, that man, curled up on the ground' Jack says 'with is nose all bloody but e darent get up!'

'and' says the kid in the grass 'es making a crocodile noise!'

so we strike some matches and suck hard on our woodbines to keep them alight,

everythings closed Sunday afternoon so we go down the back of the Gaumont and im telling Mike and Di all about the horror film i saw and we climb over the brick wall and into the yard,

'give me a leg up' i ask Mike,

and he does because the walls quite high,

'now me' Di says,

and he comes last,

so we open up the huge dustbins where we find all sorts of things because what we are after is bits of film that got chucked out and there are generally lots of them and each one is a strip of tiny pictures and sometimes you can stretch your arms wide and see the whole thing, and we look for the film stars we know and Alan Ladd is my favourite because hes the nicest but Mikes is Rita Hayworth, and we roll up whatever we can find to keep, so we have lots of pictures of men with women that we can take home, and another thing is the huge light bulbs that are useless and burnt out because we chuck these against the wall to hear them *POP*, but if anyone walks past the gates we have to hide and wait till theyve gone, except if its other kids in the back lane and then we chuck a couple of the bulbs over the top and we hear them go off and the kids run away,

and the hairdresser lets me sit here when theres a huge sort of half-egg thing over Mums head that swallows her up while she reads a magazine like nothings happened at all,

'you could have knocked me over with a feather' says one lady,

'well i never!' says another,

and the ladies have to sit still with their hair full of tin clips and rollers, and the chairs swivel on the spot while the hairdressers get round them with their scissors snippering,

'you wouldnt read about it!' says Mum reading,

and her hairdresser says 'and i said, who says? i said'

and she crosses over to the gas ring to take some long tongs off the flame and she goes for Mum till her heads smoking and she curls her hair some more and now it really stinks and spray gets squirted around, and when another customer pokes her nose in to take a look at the queue the clumps of hair all roll across the floor away from the door,

'i shall call back later' says the lady in the doorway 'toodle-oo'

and another one under a half-egg thing comes out and i can see its Mrs Harris with her hair bright ginger, and there are mirrors all over the place so you can watch the back of everybodys head and there are little jars of nail polish standing in a row, and while one ladys doubled over a washbasin someone foams up the shampoo so i wonder why she doesnt wash her own hair like i can do mine, but Mums told me that this is where film stars come when they want to look beautiful because they have to put their heads under these things first and hold out their hands one finger at a time for the red to be painted on, and Mums having hers painted because tonight shes going out, so she fans the air with her hands because the hairdressers is full of this smell of hot hair and perfume and stuff,

'would you rather play in the street, darling?' she says to me and she looks at the colour on her nails,

'i like it here' i tell her,

and the hairdresser looks up at me in the mirror and gives me a special smile,

and i should tell you that its a big thing when Mum goes out and i think going outs what she likes to do most of all, while we three stay over with Gran and we take our ludo and our Monopoly to the little house she lives in now,

Pam shares a desk with me, but i dont know whether its alright to have a girl for a best friend and especially in the break when sometimes she does knitting instead of joining in tag and Roger Sawyer doesnt like her but Mike says a girl can be your best friend if you kiss her,

down by the railway tracks we are watching two engines pull a freight train along and its loaded with army tanks all in a line gliding smoothing past us and there are covers on the big guns and the ground rumbles and we wait to see them go to London and on our way home we fossick around in the coal pits to steal as much as we can hide in our pockets, but we have to sneak into the flat and mix the stolen lumps with the coal already in the scuttle because Mum mustnt find out or shed make us take it all back, and anyway weve got to have it because of the cold at night and theres been no parcels from Australia for ages so we dont know what to do for something special,

Allan Patterson is my new friend but Mum says he spells his name wrong because Allan should have only one *l* and Patterson should have one *t*,

'but how can he be *wrong* about his name?' i say,

and anyhow i like Patterson because we talk about everything and sometimes when he wheels his bike along the road we walk home together and he shows me the little garden at the side of his house on Bristol Road and thats where we stand talking and getting cold, but sometimes Patterson sounds just like an old man,

'the garden gets the morning sun' he says,

and i can see a garden fork stuck in a pile of cow poo,

'youve a lot of things growing' i say,

'my dad does it all' he says,

'your *dad*?'

and so theres something wrong if his dad is here and Patterson takes his glasses off to rub them clean on his shirt,

'hes too sick to go to the war' he says,

and i look up at the sky between the chimneys,

'you lucky thing, Patterson!' i tell him '*we* live in a flat'

and in the yard he keeps mice so thats what he smells of, and he points to a potato plant and two lettuces,

'this bits mine' he says and takes me right up close to look,

so now i hate him,

but he sticks a hand in his pocket to pull out a mess of string,

'you hold one end' he says,

and he gets busy and when theres a good long straight bit he lays it out on the dirt,

'this can be your corner' he says,

'but you mean—?'

and Patterson says 'you can grow what you like'

and i dont know what to say so i get out all the marbles ive got in my pocket to give to him but he shakes his head,

'go on' says Patterson 'dig your fingers in'

so i break a clod with my thumbs,

'here' Patterson says 'try Dads spade and dig a hole'

and the spades too big but the earth is easy and the smell reminds me of the woods when i make a hole and now i can look down into it and Patterson slings his jacket across his shoulders,

'when you finish you have to stand the spade against the wall over here' he says,

and i say 'okay'

and Patterson says 'it belongs right under the bathtub'

and i say 'okay' getting a good look at a grey tin bath hung up on a nail 'is that a real bath?'

'what does it look like?'

'do you use it?' i say,

'of course we do' Patterson says,

'in the bathroom?' i say,

'in the kitchen' Patterson says and he takes a turn at digging my corner of his garden,

and Mrs Patterson comes to the window so she can watch but when i wave to her she goes away,

'so what happens if your dad comes home now' i ask 'and blows you up?'

'what for?' says Patterson,

i dont like to explain that me being here is wrong,

'is he old?' i say because anyway im thinking about the war and everything,

'he commands the Home Guard' Patterson says 'and hes head of the Invasion Committee'

so this is my lucky day,

'can i have a ride on your bike?' i say,

Patterson thinks about it,

'no' he says,

on the brewery sign theres a dead sheep hung up by a strap round its middle and this is the beer im going to drink when im a man and the whole brewery smells strong and *sour* even with rain coming down and puddles in the street,

'i know you!' the policeman shouts,

and i jump a mile,

and hes standing in the rain propping up his bicycle,

'ive had my eye on you' the policeman says,

so he must have found out about the flour mill!

'youre the lad rattling a stick along the fence in Butchers Lane' the policeman says,

'no im not'

and Dis voice comes from a long way off 'get a *move* on, Rod!'

‘thats my sister and shes waiting for me’ i explain ‘and our mum works at the Ministry of Food’

the policemans helmet and his cape are soaking wet and shiny,

‘well, perhaps i shall let you off this time’ he says,

and suddenly he laughs and hes happy but i dont get why,

‘so hop it’ he says,

‘yes’ i say and my cap drips and my teeth are chattering,

‘but dont let me catch you malingering again’ he laughs,

and this is a new word like trespassers that im going to remember for school,

ma-ling-gering,

i get a creepy idea that an X-ray is looking through my whole body and ive turned invisible green, but if *soldiers* could be invisible theyd help win the war, and this is such a great idea i tell Di,

‘then what about invisible enemy commandos!’ Di says ‘prowling around town with their guns all ready to shoot us and no one even knowing’

‘but wouldnt we see the *guns*’ i say ‘floating up and down the street?’

and the radio is on while we eat tea though Mum calls tea dinner,

'dinners in the middle of the day' i tell her 'everybody knows that'

'dont put your elbows on the table' she says,

but the Workers Playtime music suddenly stops right in the middle of a song and a posh gentlemans voice comes on,

'this is your English friend in Germany' the voice says,

and Mums face goes white and her knuckles too because she has to hold on to the table,

'the bombing has done terrible things to you' says the radio 'and we know that panic is breaking out, well this is all because your government tells lies to stop you finding out that youre losing the war, and youve been losing since Poland fell and then France fell and next it will be Britains turn'

Mum screws her face up,

'what?' says Mike looking interested,

'the British lion is wounded' says the gentlemans voice 'and soon enough it will be all over, but this need never happen because the English people and German people are cousins and we should be allies not enemies'

but Mum leaps to her feet and up out of her chair and she knocks her cup where it smashes on the lino in a puddle of tea and its a good cup too,

'so why fight against what—' says the voice,

'you *traitor*!' Mum shrieks at the set and snaps it off,

and i know all about traitors and deserters too but i never expected a traitor on our radio in our own flat,

'that man' she turns round to face us before she speaks 'is Lord Haw-Haw!'

and her look shows how horrible this is,

'do they have Lord Haw-Haw in Kangaroo Valley?' i ask,

'what on earth makes you ask a question like that?' she says,

and suddenly she rushes over and she holds me by the ears and kisses my hair,

and Joan gives me a book called Pinocchio to read out of so she can teach me how to speak properly and this is called elocution, but i dont get past Once upon a Time because i cant seem to say Time the way she wants,

'teim' Joan says to show me and i watch her teeth,

'time'

'teim'

'time'

she sighs at last and lets me read the next bit thats about a piece of wood speaking when the carpenter cuts it, which is why he makes it into a puppet instead of making it into a table leg and he calls this puppet Pinocchio and there are all sorts of words i am supposed to pay attention to if im to speak properly like that traitor, but the only thing i can think about is the talking wood saying 'teim',

and Joan tells me she isnt speaking to Gran, except to say yes or no.

and the biggest thing now is adding up all our pennies and half-pennies plus several sixpences earned from Gran for running errands and even for just promising to love her, so Michael can go out to buy the glider kit from the hobby shop because hes fourteen and thats old enough, and the kits called the Dove and its made of balsa wood,

and this kit belongs to me as well because it belongs to us all,

'before the war your Uncle Ralph used to fly a glider' Mum says 'a real one'

and we get straight to work on the Dove and on the box theres a picture of it so we can see what it will look like when its finished and the three of us sit round the kitchen table unfolding the plan printed on a big sheet of paper and spreading it out flat, and we get everything needed because there has to be glue and razor blades and scissors and pins, and what you do is match the little balsa wood shapes to the drawing on the plan and then fix them together to make a frame, and Mike reads out the instructions,

'it says here to build the fuselage first and the tail next and the wing last'

'why?' i say,

'because' says Mike,

and the tip of Dis tongue shows because she has to concentrate on what shes doing,

'whatre these for?' i ask and hold up two rubber bands,

'we use them later' Mike says,

and we make a start on cutting out components and constructing the frame from long strips as thin as matchsticks, but the wood can split so you have to be careful,

'balsa wood is the worlds lightest wood' Mike tells us,

and while we work he talks to us about aerofoils and how the wind passes over the aerofoil to give the glider *lift* because now weve got a whole lot of new words, and Mike even draws the wind for us like a lot of hair, but the cutting and glueing are slow jobs and its important to follow the numbers printed on the wood because they have to match the plan,

'and then we can glue the bits together and put them aside to dry' Mike says,

but i make a dreadful mistake,

'you clot!' Mike shouts,

because im cutting around the shape of an aerofoil and its gone wonky and now i can see for myself and all i do is stare at it through my tears and everythings spoilt because nobody can ever put back the curved bit that just got just cut off, but Mike comes to the rescue because he bought a spare sheet of balsa and he cuts the right shape so now the wrecked one can be thrown out,

'you can start putting the fuselage together from all these square cross-sections weve made, if you like' Mike says,

and this is better because i know to start with the nose-block and that the square sections get bigger and bigger up to where the cockpit fits in and theres even a little mica cut-out for the windscreen, then the sections taper down to reach the tail,

'the tail assembly and the wings need to be made separately' says Mike reading off the plan,

and i *know* but i dont say anything because hes being nice and the frame im glueing up looks right and this is even better than meccano,

'when its dry can we add the tail fin on?' i say,

'thats going to be my job' says Di,

'look at this!' Mike says because he has got the wing skeleton done,

and it sits on the table with both ends tilting up at the tips,

so we cut some sheets of tissue-paper and we glue them on in panels, and now the whole model is white and begins to look exactly like a real plane and the edges get trimmed with scissors and finally some water gets flicked all over it so the paper dries tight like a drum,

'its time for your rubber bands' Mike tells me and he takes them off me and straps the wings on,

and the Dove is bigger than i thought and stronger than anything,

and Mum comes to look and she promises to take us all up to the fort on the common for the maiden flight,

lying on my back theres warm grass and theres the sky thats nothing but blue, and the blues so deep i can look right in and theres a vapour trail like a straight line drawn with chalk getting wider and *ripply* at one end so that it turns into a feather,

'of *course* i shall come right to the top with you' Mum says 'i need a break from worry'

and now we take turns carrying the Dove because up here we can look right across the whole hillside and the wind blows the grass flat to the ground and theres nobody else so weve got the place to ourselves,

'this is a lucky day' Mike says,

'i can feel God' Di says,

'what nonsense, darling' Mum says 'is that what Gran told you?'

so i try to see if i can feel God too, but its just something blowing around my knees,

'perfect flying conditions' Michael says 'just look at the downdraught!'

and tiny spring flowers all around us are nodding in among the grass and the blue ones are harebells,

'what about here?' Mum says,

so we put our basket down right by the wall of the fort and everywheres warm,

'theres a joke' i tell them 'i say *knock knock* and then you say *whos there?* and then i say *Lydia* and then you have to say *Lydia who?*'

but they just stand like idiots looking at me,

'well?' i say,

and then Mum gets it,

'Lydia who?' she says,

and i say 'Lydia Dustbin!'

and Mum laughs but the others take no notice and its them i was really telling,

'if you watch the sky' Mike says 'you can feel the world rising under your feet' and i try but it doesnt work,

and i put my face against the ground because even thats warm,

'the flight of the Dove!' Mike says,

'so whos going to launch it?' Di asks,

'me' i say and i jump up,

'why is it always you?' Di says,

'anyway' Michael says 'scientifically it should be someone who can be trusted not to crash it the very first time'

but im sick of science,

'Mum has to choose who' i say,

but Mum plants herself on the blanket and begins unpacking the picnic lunch,

'you *have to*' Di tells her,

'yes' Mike and i say together 'come on Mum'

and Mum stops what shes doing with a look of delight and she dusts the crumbs off her skirt and gets up and reaches for the glider,

'but—' i say,

and she takes hold of the Dove the way Mike shows her, so nothing can stop her now and we have to make the best of it, so we give her a few tips to be sure she gets the idea because grown-ups dont know the same stuff as kids,

'like this?' Mum checks and she holds our glider above her head with its white wings like a crown 'am i doing alright, darlings?'

so she draws back her arm ready,

and Mike takes hold of her shoulders from behind and he turns her to face the wind,

she hardly seems to throw it at all but the Dove rises

all by itself, higher and higher till it seems to stand still in the sky, and thats what ive been hoping for and then it dips and steers itself and floats and swoops,

'lovely!' Mum says 'how lovely!'

and we all stand with our backs to the fort to watch it,

'thats our Dove' i say,

'*flying*' Di says,

and weve done it!

'look out!' i say because it banks away across the hillside,

'thats okay' Mike says and grins,

and lower and lower the Dove glides until it skims along on the grass,

'perfect' Mike says 'a perfect landing and a perfect maiden flight'

and Mum looks pleased,

'whos next?' she says,

but by the time *my* turn comes the gliders nose is streaked with grass stains but i rush to pick it up and point it into the wind and raise it above my head like Mum did and already i can feel it lifting and trying to escape so i hold tight,

'good luck, darling!' Mum calls,

and im on tiptoe running with it, running into the wind and down the hill and this flight is going to be better than anyone elses because thats my plan, but my fingers let go before im really ready, 'damn!' i say,

the Dove hesitates,

and its wings tilt,

and up goes the nose!

and it swerves and crashes to the ground tumbling nose over tail, and Michael groans because the wings are knocked crooked,

'that wasnt a proper go' i yell 'so ive got to have another!'

but Mike shakes his head and gets busy fixing the elastic band to put the wings right,

'four flights are enough for now anyway and at least we now know its strong enough to crash' says Mum and delves into the basket 'so shall we try Winifreds pineapple?'

and she gets to work on the pineapple can with the tin opener,

'i dont want any' i tell her,

'alright, but just taste a smidgen so we can thank her properly, and then you neednt have a second piece'

so i let her spoon some between my lips and the most amazing taste fills my mouth,

'wow!' i say when ive swallowed,

'so?' says Mike 'what?'

'i thought it was going to be apples' i say,

Mike tells me a secret while we carry the shopping home,

'i shall design my own glider' he says 'a huge glider with a six-foot wing-span'

'a sail-plane?' i say,

'yes and im going to cut the aerofoils deeper and more curved than anybody ever before, and im going to add a couple of degrees to the tilted wingtips *and* im going to enlarge the tail'

this is so important that we walk together to think about it,

'you want to know something else?' he says,

'yes' i say,

'ive been reading about dead bodies' he says 'and even while a man is in his coffin buried underground his hair keeps growing'

'what hair?' i screech,

'his hair, you know' he says 'all of it'

'on his arms?' i say,

'yes and his face too'

'and his chest?'

and Mike nods,

'all of it' he says,

my shoes click because of the new studs the shoemaker hammered into the toes and heels and i walk so i sound like a soldier and Patterson checks on them because he wants the same,

'i got some Yates seeds' i tell him,

and we kneel down together to begin my very first garden because all i ever grew before is mustard and cress at home, and the packet says to plant the seeds half an inch underground with ten inches between, but Pattersons dad comes out to watch and he takes hold of the packet to get a close look,

'lupins' i say,

'i can read well enough' says Mr Patterson 'but flowers are no use to anyone' and he points at Allan with the garden fork in his hand,

'so what are *you* planting?'

'marrows, Dad'

'now thats a good choice' Mr Patterson says 'because marrows keep producing more and more marrows'

but i dont like to say that i hate marrows anyway and when Mum stuffs and cooks them in the oven id rather just eat the breadcrumbs and herbs out of the middle and leave the sloppy marrow part, even though Gran says there are millions of starving people in the world who would be more grateful than me,

'not like cabbages' Mr Patterson says 'once you cut a cabbage its cut'

and he and Patterson begin digging side by side,

so Patterson says 'Hall lives in a flat'

and his dad looks at me,

'i like flowers' i say,

a doctor comes to the school but its not Dr Halliday because this ones a free doctor whos going to give us all the examination and its my turn in the line,

'take off your pullover and your shirt' the nurse says 'good, and your shoes and socks, good, and your shorts too, and go over there to the doctor so he can listen to your chest'

but i wont take off my shorts,

'take off your shorts, please' says the nurse 'you are allowed to keep your underpants on'

but i cant tell her that i dont have any underpants,

'take those shorts *off*!' the nurse says,

and i wont because i didnt know you had to wear underpants, and i dont have any,

'never mind, nurse, we cant wait a month, send him over just as he is' the doctor says 'i dont have time'

'teim' i whisper,

but he puts some cold thing on my chest and my back and tells me to cough and suddenly im frightened of what he can hear inside me that i dont know about.

9

All the kids are screaming round the playground but i find Patterson crying behind the bicycle shed and his hanky is all stuck together with snot,

'you cant come round to my house anymore' he says 'cos my mums ill'

'what sort of ill?' i say,

'shes going to have a baby'

'thats terrible' i say,

'and she doesnt want it' Patterson says,

'you could run away' i say,

'i think i will and all' he says,

'as long as your dad doesnt catch you' i say,

'*he* doesnt want the baby either' Patterson says,

so i put my arm round his shoulder like Mike sometimes puts his round me,

'and *i* dont want it!' Patterson says,

so everybody doesnt want that baby and Patterson sticks his fists in his pockets and he gets out from under my arm,

and i cant wait till its safe to jump down out of the green bus but Olive takes longer because she gets puffed,

'come on, Aunty!' i say,

and its so windy i have to button up my jacket, but the last two buttons that havent fallen off are in the wrong place,

'oh! what a beautiful old house!' says Olive 'wild horses in a blizzard wouldnt keep me from this sale!'

and that gets me giggling because here come the wild horses pulling one way and Olive pulling the other and a tremendous struggles going on,

'first thing' she tells me 'we shall need to register' so she goes up to a lady sitting under a garden umbrella,

'heres your card then' says the lady 'and your catalogue'

and Olive gets a big number 138 and she turns to me and gives me the catalogue to carry,

'from now on' she says 'you can be in charge'

so i say 'thank you' to the lady,

and i take hold of Olives hand and lead her up some steps that are a mile wide,

'what do you think?' Olive says,

'smashing' i say,

and inside the whole place is full of things with numbers stuck on them and there are lots of people walking around on the stone floor and up above theres an empty stairway with about a thousand stairs and a curly banister, but nobody seems to be talking to anybody, so something must be wrong,

and i tug Olives sleeve and whisper 'is someone dead?'

'*no,* pet!' she says 'well *yes* but not right now'

and i wish there was because the only time i ever saw anyone dead was animals,

'look at this, Aunty!' i say 'what is it?'

'its an umbrella stand' she says 'number 1127'

i run my finger down the page till i find what im looking for because im a good reader like Great-Uncle Mont says,

'its an *elephants foot*'

'such big horny toenails' Olive says 'and once upon a time somebody had to hollow that out'

but what would the elephant do without a foot? and i remember a creepy film i once saw about a man with a statues leg,

'how?' i say,

'i expect they killed it for the ivory first' she says,

'are we going to buy it?' i ask,

'can you imagine' says Olive 'what my *mother* would say!'

and i do see Mrs Freestone catching sight of the elephants foot standing by itself at the front door and going '*WHAT IN—!*' but a lady wearing a hat leans across in front of me and reaches for the label thats got its number on, like she cant read without sticking her face where it isnt wanted, 'but how about this!' Olive says 'isnt this the very thing for *you*?'

because up on the wall theres a real sword,

i tell her 'that leather things called a scabbard, Aunty'

'so it is, dear' she says,

and here i come, so watch out! swinging this sword around my head and im up on a horse and theres a battle going on and im the captain and there are men in helmets swarming around me and lots of dust in the air and we are all on horses and i point with my sword and i shout *Charge!*

'lets mark it in the catalogue and see how the bidding goes' Olive says 'because you never can tell'

so we find the sword on the list and i give it a tick, but theres no point really because a swords something i could never hope to own when i dont even have a bicycle,

'such a lot of people! one can scarcely breathe!' Olive says fanning herself 'itll be pandemonium once the auctioner begins'

and we set off to explore some other rooms, and in the kitchen i poke my nose into some huge pots and theres a weird-looking mincer that must be *prehistoric*,

'do you think my Gran would like this?' i ask,

and Olive nods 'theres a lot your Gran would like'

and heaps of wooden spoons and sieves and things are all tied together in bundles and people stand round looking at them and making marks in their catalogues, but Olive isnt interested even though the plates are not chipped like ours at home, so she says we should head for the ballroom instead or the library because shes determined to find something that she says is unusual and she reads aloud from the catalogue,

'the Grange has thirty-two rooms' she reads 'but the upstairs is closed to the public'

'okay' i say,

and in the music room she sits on a piano stool as if shes going to play,

'i shall catch my breath here' she says,

and she opens the lid to look at the keys,

'we hide under our piano' i tell her,

'and do you mean to say your mother cant find you?'

'she hides *with* us'

and Olive nods 'Dods is such a sport' she says,

but i go scouting because i think ive found somewhere interesting and i report back to Olive,

'good for you, darling' she says 'i shall join you soon though dont go far'

and in here theres a huge green table and a little blackboard that someones been writing on with chalk,

'now then, laddie' says a man with a badge 'dont touch'

'i wasnt going to' i say,

so i keep going straight through and out into a room crammed with a million books and WOW! something else, because the glass cases are filled with *hundreds* and *hundreds* of butterflies and moths,

'lovely little chaps, arent they?' says a parson in a collar and he looks down at me over the top of his glasses 'are you interested in butterflies?'

'yes thank you' i say,

and he gets another good look at me,

'so grave' he says 'and so correct'

and he lends me this big magnifying glass hes got so i can bring them up close, and i know all about magnifying glasses because we use ours for stamps, but when i move my head something happens that ive never seen before because on these butterflies the blue *changes* like the wings are alive,

'of course we have our own beauties in the British Isles' the parson says 'the swallowtail for instance'

'and the peacock' i say,

'yes indeed, but nothing quite so handsome as these, i think'

and i say 'these are better than anything'

and i want the butterflies so much im going to burst, but suddenly i remember that ive forgotten Clive, so i give back the magnifying glass,

'i have to find my aunty' i tell him,

and he pats me on the head and wanders away, and *why* ive got to find Olive is that someone else may get in first and buy these butterflies before we can, but,

but, what if im too late already? what if i catch up with her and bring her back, only to find theyve been sold already? wont it be safer to *take* them to her? i mean just the blue ones?

'excuse me' i say,

because i have to reach between some people looking at the moths, and ever so carefully i pick up the glass case i want,

'pardon' i say because a crowd comes in all of a sudden and its a bit hard to see my way past the wooden frame im carrying, though Olive never goes far off so she should be easy to find,

'oops!' i say,

and i bump into an old lady on the way,

'what on earth!' she says,

but i cant bother with her because im too terrified of dropping the case,

'now now' says a mans voice behind me 'where in the world might you be going with those splendid specimens?'

but im in the middle of wangling them through the doorway,

'i have to look for my aunty' i explain,

and i hang on tight to the butterflies, but now i see its only the parson and hes my friend,

'well' he says 'i think youd better let me lend you a hand'

'i want her to buy them' i tell him,

'theyll be quite safe' he says 'where they belong'

and he takes hold of the frame and gets it off me and he lifts it way up out of my reach, but thats when i notice one of the butterflies has fallen off the display and the whole things wrecked, though i dont know whether it was his fault or mine and anyway i dont think he knows yet,

'follow me' he says,

and thats lucky because now im scared that sooner or later hes going to see the fallen butterfly and i dont want to be arrested, so i let him go first and leave him to it and i duck off the opposite way instead, around corners and in along the corridor among people peering at things on tables, and here comes Olive in a fluster looking all ways at once,

'where *were* you?' she says 'you gave me such a fright'

and she pats her bosom and she kisses and kisses me,

'i was just looking for you' i say,

'heaven knows' she says 'how i would have explained to your dear mother'

and she tucks my hand under her arm and turns me round and leads me back the way ive come,

'but down there theres nothing' i tell her 'only a whole lot of dusty old books'

and luckily she stops on the way to look at some hairbrushes and clocks and razors and starched collars and stuff so i point out that the clocks are still ticking, 'oh!' says Olive 'should i go for this?'

but its only a handbag with a sparkly clip,

'i dont like it' i tell her,

'alright, pet' Olive says,

and she puts it back,

'now i happen to know that just in here' and she reaches for a doorknob 'is a surprise'

'what is it?' i say,

'something so *extravagant* youll never guess' she says,

and we go in,

'this was the family chapel' she says,

and i can smell burnt candles and its all quiet because theres nobody else around except an old lady in a black hat sitting on a pew who takes no notice of us and we take no notice of her,

'just look!' Olive whispers,

so i do,

'what do you think?' Olive whispers,

'golly!' i whisper back,

because its a huge contraption with twisty gold pillars and an empty picture frame and a statue on top and the whole thing must weigh a *ton*,

Olive says 'isnt he gorgeous!'

i ask 'but whats it *for*?'

and Olive says 'this is an altar' and she gets busy with her spectacles 'but theyve given it a number so it must be for sale!'

'who is that man?' i whisper,

'well, pet, hes killing a dragon so he must be Saint George or Saint Michael'

and she looks in the catalogue, but what im thinking is *Saint* Michael!

and Olive whispers 'yes its Saint Michael and apparently there was once a painting of the Virgin Mary too but shes already been sold'

i get a good look at him wearing a golden kilt, and his shiny legs are amazingly muscly,

'do you suppose?' says Olive still whispering and she glances back over her shoulder because i suppose she doesnt want the lady to overhear 'do you think my ceilings at New Mills Court would be high enough?'

'youre not going to *buy* it, Aunty!'

Olive clasps her hands and says 'its so wonderfully Catholic, you must admit'

and i can see she loves it,

'is Uncle Ralph going to like it too?' i ask,

'now theres a thought' she says,

so i have a really good look to see if i can guess,

and the gold glimmers,

'it may cost a lot of money' i warn her,

'no one else seems much interested' Olive says,

and the lady behind us quietly blows her nose,

'thats the beauty of sales' Olive whispers,

but right then a whole lot of people come in to look,

'bad luck' i whisper,

'this piece' says a voice sounding loud behind us 'was imported from Italy'

and its my parson holding his hat in his hand, so i try to hide behind Olive so he wont see me but he smiles and comes over to join us looking at Saint Michael,

'i should warn you' he says to Olive 'that our young friend here has his eye on a collection of Ulysses butterflies'

Olive looks surprised,

'oh yes, we met in the library, he and i' he tells her 'and we had a good talk'

'really?' she says,

'yes and i must say its heartening' he says 'to find a boy who shares my enthusiasm for Australia'

but how does he know about Australia?

'im afraid i dont understand' Olive says,

nor me,

'the Ulysses is a beautiful little creature found in the north of that country' he tells her 'you should take a look at them, madam, though im afraid the whole collection may be something of a prize and destined for a museum'

and of all the things i ever dreamt about Australia i never once thought about butterflies, and he gets talking to Olive and they make their way back to the library and ive got no way out, so here we are again and im sure my face has already gone red because that fallen butterfly is still lying on its side at the bottom of the frame and my eyes wont look at anything else,

'how sweet they are!' Olive says,

but i can feel tears coming so i escape across the room and pretend to study a map thats big and shiny and coloured pink with cracks in the varnish and up the top it says *NEW SOUTH WALES*, so now i cant believe my luck, and the places on it have such funny names i get out my autograph book to write them down in the back for Mum, *Wagga Wagga, Wollongong,*

and the parson comes to look over my shoulder,

'are you something of a scholar as well, then, old chap?' he says,

suddenly i point,

'Kangaroo Valley!' i say and it comes out as a shout,

the parson steps back in surprise and looks up at the map,

'quaint indeed' he says,

'thats where Mum found the giant ant-hill' i say 'and they rode horses and sat round the fire and—and—'

but Olive is still looking at the butterflies and she calls me over,

'the blue changes when you move, Rodney' she says to me 'do you see that?' and she murmurs 'so luminous'

and im going to remember this word too.

and i can see our reflection in the glass with Olives

face close up beside mine, her in her goggles and me in my school cap,

'but what a pity one has fallen off' she says,

Pam painted a princess picture in purple and green ready for Mr Marks and she showed me so i told Mike about it and i asked him if she could come along next time we play in the flour mill, but Mike said no,

and now Allans here balancing on the wooden fence at the side of the graveyard and he calls out to me like he always does,

'wotcher, cock!'

i say 'wotcher, cock!' back at him because Mums nowhere round to hear me,

i get an idea and id like to know if my idea is a good one so i whisper across the dark bedroom,

'Mike, are you awake?'

and after a while Mike says 'maybe yes and maybe no'

'ive got an idea'

and i tell him my idea that blowing up Mr Sawyers house would be more difficult than building it,

'why? Mike says,

so i say 'if you have to *invent* the bomb! and—'

Mike flings his sheet off,

'—and if you have to drop it from a plane so that it *hits* the house' i tell him and this sounds like science to me,

'and' i think of something else '*and* if you have to invent the *plane!* too'

Mike doesnt laugh at me the way he did when i was little,

so i whisper 'are you asleep again?'

but now he sits up in bed and hes staring at me in the moonlight,

with this mist today everythings damp and the grounds all soggy and my shoes leak because the soles are worn out, everythings gone wrong now the holidays are finished and we have to go back to school and Dis marching on ahead so im all alone and i turn back to look for what i just lost, and i look and i kick the ground and this is the *end*,

Joan and Ken are home,

and Gran calls them the Honeymoon Couple,

'whats a honeymoon?' i ask Mum,

but shes busy in the kitchen cutting Xs into the bottom of Brussels sprouts,

'whats a honeymoon?' i ask again,

'you go on a honeymoon when youre first married' she says,

and i get it, like a bus,

'are Joan and Ken coming round for tea?' i ask,

'they were expected a quarter of an hour ago' she says,

so i lend a hand helping to peel some potatoes,

'whys Joan our only real aunt?' i say,

'shes not, theres all that *Hall* family' she tells me 'because Dick had sisters, and brothers too, but they never get in touch'

'dont they like us?' i ask,

'some of them do' she says 'Gertrude does and so does Alice'

'then why dont *they* talk to us?' i say,

'maybe theyre too busy' Mum says,

'what, always?' i say,

'and theyre all so much older than Dick was and Dick was seventeen years older than me' Mum says 'so we have nothing in common and they live in London anyway'

'but if we write to them' i suggest 'they might send us birthday presents'

'do stop pestering me' Mum says 'i fell out with them years ago and thats that'

so the kitchen goes quiet and the taps running,

'anyway' Mum says 'youll have a new cousin soon'

'how?'

'Joans having a baby'

'so is she *ill*?' i say,

'good heavens, no' says Mum,

and Joan comes in looking happy so we sit in the lounge while Mums cooking, and weve got a jigsaw puzzle already half finished on the card table,

'if its a boy we shall call him Andrew' Joan tell us,

and she goes out to fetch some tea while Ken makes himself at home on the settee watching us and our Dutch houses picture thats not finished,

'Ken' Di says 'do you want to help?'

'you cant call me Ken anymore' he tells her 'you have to call me *Uncle* Ken'

but Diana looks bold,

'that sounds silly!' she says,

'only because youre a spoilt brat' Ken says,

and i begin to wish Mum wasnt out in the kitchen working,

'i am not spoilt!' Di says and she can, because she knows shes Kens favourite,

and Joan comes in with the tray,

'we never call Joan *Aunty* Joan' Mike says.

and Joan smiles and pours the tea,

'who takes milk and who takes sugar?' she says,

but of course everyone knows what everyone has and

for instance i know that she likes hers really strong with just a pinch of sugar on the tip of the spoon,

'one sugar for Ken' Di says when she passes him his cup and saucer,

but he bangs it straight down on the table and hes up on his feet and his face is all bristly and he catches Di under the armpits and slings her across his knee, and i cant believe, but already hes spanking her and it must hurt because she goes bright red,

'stop!' i yell,

but Di wriggles free and races down the passage,

'you beast!' she yells at him, then we hear the bedroom door slam

and i hope he doesnt pick on me next,

and next thing Mum comes out of the kitchen and goes flying past, Mike bends over the puzzle and helps me find the piece of sky i need and Joan sips her tea, and the bedroom door opens again and closes, and now Mum comes in and anybody can see shes furious,

'Diana has welts on her bottom' she says 'and on her thigh as well'

and Joan gives a little cry, but Kens got his arms spread along the back of the settee,

'dont you dare!' Mum says to him 'dont you ever dare lay a hand on any of my children again'

'someone has to teach her manners' Ken says 'shes allowed to run wild' and he adds 'they all are' and i can hear Diana sobbing in the bedroom,

Mum looks like a bomb thats about to go off,

'i shall not ask you to apologise to her' she says 'that would be expecting too much, but neither shall i expect *her* to forgive you'

Ken gets to his feet and hes huge and his black moustache is huge and his Hitler hair flops over his brow,

holding the teapot Joan sits with tears in her eyes,

and still the sobbing in the bedroom goes on,

now Ken sticks his army cap on his head and he stuffs his fingers in his leather gloves and sticks his swagger-stick under his arm and his Sam Browne creaks and he strides out through the kitchen and away across the yard and down our outside stairs he goes,

and i hope he never comes back,

its my turn to light the fire and this is one job i enjoy because i like making spills, spitting on one corner of a sheet of newspaper to start rolling it nice and tight until the whole things a long stick that you can loop around into a flat knot, though sometimes we use kindling instead, if weve collected enough in the woods or if Mum paid the gypsies for some, and i like cleaning the grate out and stacking small bits of coal on and some of this is railway coal, and i like striking matches, but this fire wont catch so i try our usual trick to help it draw by holding an open newspaper across the mouth of the fireplace till the big sheet gets sucked flat, and the power of it begins to work when a draught rushes underneath and the paper glows brighter and brighter and now the fire roars and shows through, so this is my moment to whip it safely away,

'crikey!'

because the whole thing catches with a *whoosh* and i let go, and the newpaper blazes and folds inwards and the chimney gobbles it up, and i leap clear and dust my hands,

'whats up?' Mike calls from the kitchen,

'fires going' i say,

anyhow tomorrows my turn for washing up and thats no fun at all, so i make the most of the fire now and i get ready to put some coal on, but several red-hot lumps of soot come tumbling down from the chimney right out of the fireplace and bounce across the carpet so i have to go for them with the tongs,

'help!' i yell,

Mike leaps in through the door and snatches up the shovel and begins smothering the fire in the fireplace and the whole room fills up with smoke because its burning so well, and his eyes are streaming and mine too,

'the chimneys on fire' Mike says,

'so what do we *do*?'

'we have to wait till Mum comes home to find out if we need to call the fire brigade'

the fire brigade!

'in Kangaroo Valley' i yell at Mike 'fires get lit in the open air and people sit round them on the ground and—and—they kill things and stick them on the flames and eat them—and—chop down trees and shoot snakes and drink tea.'

'forget it!' Mike snaps, looking scared,

and suddenly the whole things awful,

'no good blubbering' Mike says,

and the frog i keep in my pocket squirms and feels heavy,

the ground crackles under our feet because of the frosty crust, so its fun to listen to ourselves *tramping* out of the woods and on to the road and we can set off home now because we cant manage anymore than weve got and *what* weve got is a whole lot of ivy pulled down off the trees and big bundles of holly that even have a few red berries that are hard to find and some mistletoe too, so i start singing now im happy,

'Hark the herald angels sing' i sing because its my favourite,

and the others join in and all the way to town we sing

and everyone in the whole world can hear and they can see where weve been and Roger is out in the street all got up in his balaclava and overcoat,

'why didnt you tell me you were going to the woods?' he shouts,

'sorry, Roger' says Mike 'do you want to come home with us?'

'i cant, im waiting for Dad'

'lets go' i say because i dont want Roger hanging around 'its started spitting'

'Christmas comes but once a year!' the fish lady says when we turn in along the lane like an army and march past tramping in time with the music right to our stairs and all the way to the top and the ivys so late coming behind us that its still only halfway up, and lots of raindrops start pattering on the iron roof,

'a good job we kept going' Di says,

and the delicious smell from the kitchen is Mums Christmas cooking that shes doing ready for tomorrow when Joan is supposed to bring Ken round, because Ken sent Diana a doll for her birthday and hes home again on leave from the war, and when Mum opens the back door her hands are all floury but now she sees what weve got she claps just the same,

'we can do the lounge first' Mike tells her,

'well, let me know when you need me' she says 'and i shall come and help' so Di and i get busy sorting the ropes of ivy and choosing the best while Mike puts two kitchen chairs ready and he climbs up on one,

'ready, Mum' he calls,

and she comes in and stands on the other chair and we pass the ivy up and they hammer nails into the picture rail for looping the stems behind, and theres plenty of leaves to reach right round the room so our flat already begins to look like heaven,

'the pity is' says Mum 'that Christmas trees are so expensive this year'

'dont worry' says Mike up near the ceiling 'we know where to go for one'

'are you sure?' says Mum,

'and its growing wild' i tell her,

so thats why we set off with the hatchet Mike got given last year, and the tree is right beside the railway track and only about a mile away, and though its bad luck about the drizzle that cant be helped.

'therell be snow tomorrow' i say,

'no there wont' says Mike,

and we jump down into the coal pits and out along the line and when a train comes past some people wave to us out of the windows so we wave back, and we follow the tracks till we find the tree we saw and Mike lets us all have a turn at chopping but the woods too bouncy, ‘theres so much sap in the trunk’ he says,

and thats why its such hard work and even when we finish cutting the tree down its hard work, carrying it, and then its got to be hoisted up out of the coal bunker and now theres our stairs, so we are panting fit to burst at the back door, but its ours and we shake the raindrops off,

‘my, oh my!’ says Mum,

and it looks perfect between the lounge room windows because the tip just touches the ceiling, and i feel all hot and happy and wet and Mum finishes sticking some holly round the mirror over the fireplace and she hammers a nail into the door frame for the mistletoe,

‘who are you going to kiss, Mum?’ Di asks,

so Mum stops and stands there with the hammer in her hand,

but i say ‘im going to kiss Mike!’ and i make a rush for him,

‘hey!’ Mike yells and wipes my kiss off his cheek,

‘now all you need’ Mum says ‘is some colour!’

and she goes back to the kitchen to get busy rolling pastry for the mince pies while i help Di spread scissors and glue and stuff on the lounge room carpet and we begin cutting up crepe paper for making into loops for the links in a chain thats going to be long enough to cross the room from corner to corner and already we are mixing red with green, ‘afterwards’ Mike says ‘you can start cutting strips to fold across each other for the other kind of streamer’

‘stop bossing us around’ says Di,

‘thats the kind of paper chains i like best because theyre twisty’ i say,

‘well we shall hang it up in the kitchen’ says Mike,

‘why the kitchen?’ i say,

‘i can hear you’ Mum warns us,

and she bangs things around on the kitchen table,

‘anyway this glue has to dry’ Mike says ‘before we can do anything’

but i can hear Gran at the door and she arrives in a hat and overcoat with the chicken we are going to roast tomorrow so i get a good look at it and its black feathers shine green,

‘those *stairs* of yours, Dods’ says Gran ‘will be the death of me’

‘me too’ i say and i reach up to kiss her while she takes off her heavy things, and gives her scarf to me to hang up and shes puffed, but she puts an apron on straight away and sits down in the kitchen with the bird on her lap and its head dangles with a drop of blood on the beak while she begins to yank the feathers off it,

‘can i help?’ i ask

‘of course you can’ Gran says,

so we work together,

‘when did it die?’ i ask,

'last Saturday' Gran says 'and by rights we should have let it hang longer'

i get a good look at its dead eye,

'what was it like alive?' i ask,

'all cocky and full of importance and strutting around the coop' she says and she lifts one wing to get at it better,

the feathers are hard to pull out because the loose skin is too loose though i tug and tug them, and Grans much quicker than me even with her knobbly old fingers and she gets at the fluff under the wings too so theres feathers piled up on the lino and Di calls out to me from the lounge,

'its us you should be helping' she says 'with these paper chains'

'can he can finish this first, darlin?' says Gran,

and Di comes to the door,

'i suppose' she says,

'look at our chicken, Mum' i say 'how fat she is'

but Mums popping trays of mince pies in the oven,

'this ones a cockerel' Gran tells me 'its a he'

and she shoves her hand right up inside the bird and looks at the ceiling while she feels around in there to pull out long strings of bloody gizzards in her fist, and theres blood all among her knuckles,

'weve got to clean him out nice and ready for stuffin' Gran says,

and now the jobs done there are so many feathers on

the floor they bury her shoes and she holds the Christmas cockerel up by his feet,

'i dont like the look of that skin' Di says 'why cant we cook him with the feathers on?'

'the things these children think of' Gran says,

and she gets busy rubbing some lard on the bare bird,

and heres Mike blowing up our balloons so i help him now and my first balloon is a red one that im huffing and puffing into and right in front of my face it gets bigger and bigger till its bigger than my head and bigger than Gran and while i hold it steady it squeaks against my hand and now its bigger than the whole kitchen and POP!

everybody laughs but im too shocked to speak,

'you look so funny!' Di says,

'whats the matter?' Mum asks me 'it cant just be the balloon'

but i dont know and ive still got this feeling if things are loud and make me jump and i cant stop it even when someone knocks at the door,

'that must be Ken' says Gran 'since he was promoted, hes a captain'

anyway Mum goes to see, but then she steps outside and pulls the door to behind her, but a cold wind still comes in through the gap because its not quite shut and i can hear a grumbly voice out there, so i know something big is happening when i catch sight of a man with silver buttons through the door crack, but Mum still doesnt let go of the handle,

'thats as may be, Mrs Hall' says the voice 'but the fact of the matter is that your children were identified and reported'

'its Christmas!' Mum says,

'thats as may be' the policeman says again 'but the Great Western Railway has a right to protect its property'

Mum gets cross,

'so are you telling me there was a *fence* around it?'

'as to any fence i cant be sure'

'well without a Keep Out sign how can children be expected to understand?'

'howsoever' says the policeman 'i should suppose the oldest child would be the ringleader, so i can content myself with just speaking to him if you like'

'Michael' Mum calls,

and to my surprise Mikes ready and waiting like he knew something was going to happen and she opens the door to let him out into the cold,

'tsk tsk!' Gran complains because of the draught,

'Gran' i whisper 'whats going to happen?'

but she slaps the dead bird and begins packing it with stuffing,

'so let that be a warning to you, young man' the policemans voice says 'because now ive got you in my book'

and steam comes from the spout of the kettle,

'you was observed' the policemans voice says 'all three of you was observed'

'anyway when a plant grows wild' says Mum 'who is to say its not a *weed*?'

and Gran gives the cockerel a little nudge with her thumb,

'as a point of law' says the policemans voice,

'but' says Mum and now she sounds *really* cross,

'my duty' says the policemans voice,

'well all i can say' says Mum 'is that the GWR needs something better to do with its time'

'just remember this, young Michael' he says 'i shall be on the lookout for you'

'really!' says Mum 'thats too bad!'

and theres a terrible silence, so suddenly i realise Mum and Mike have been taken away from us,

at last the policeman says 'whatever your opinion Mrs Hall the railway views this as theft'

when Mum comes back in and shuts the door behind her she has her hand on Mikes shoulder,

'we shall not let this spoil our Christmas' Mum tells us all,

'is Mike going to jail?' i ask,

Mums nose is red,

'Michael was sticking up for you' she says 'and dont you forget it'

i love this moment because its morning but Mikes still asleep over there with his back to me and a Christmas stocking down near his feet, and i reach to get mine and pull it in under the eiderdown and already i can feel a ball down in the toe, but the first thing is a Dinky toy MG sports car and i wish Uncle Ralph was here and i get some coloured pencils and a twist of bullseyes and some Cadburys chocolates and some walnuts in their shells and i get my old grey socks back with the darning done so i can wear them again, but its *not* a ball at the bottom its a real orange thats heavy and too bright for anything, and i put it on my pillow right up against my nose and this is the first time i ever smelt an orange or had one in my hand, and the skin has *pores*,

and next thing Di comes racing in with her plaits flying and Mikes up now and hes got a knife that he sticks into his orange,

'Joan showed me how' he says,

so he cuts a square hole just the right size to fit a lump of sugar,

'you put your mouth here' he says 'then you squeeze and suck'

and Di looks at him over the top of her orange,

and i look at him over the top of mine and suddenly sweet juice spurts into my mouth and its the best thing,

and i get given a wooden pencil box with a lid that rolls itself away like magic when you open it,

im going to set up the biggest railway ever and our toy-chest is full of railway things that are mostly rails because Mike was given two big sets before i was born, so i begin pulling out useful parts like fork lines and level-crossings, and one set has black sleepers and one set has silver sleepers, but you can mix them up because theyre the same gauge, and each length of rail has pins and slots for fitting them together, but sometimes the pins are bent or missing so i pick out the good ones and this is a bit of a scramble because Di joins in and she says shes going to beat me and i tread on a couple of the straight tracks she has already put down,

'you did that on purpose!' she shouts,

'i did not'

'what did he do?' Mike asks,

'nothing' i say,

'yes you did' and she holds up the bent pieces,

and i hate her,

'try to be more careful' Mike tells me,

and he goes back out into the passageway to finish building a branch line that loops round towards Mums bedroom, so im going to lay mine in a circle thatll fill the whole lounge room with two stations and four signal boxes! and now its a mad scramble to get enough pieces before anyone else,

the sewing chair in Mums bedroom is an old-fashioned thing with funny little legs and drawers under the seat that swing out on hinges where Mum keeps her scissors and her cotton reels and little skeins of silk and spare zips and lots of buttons and pinking shears that Di likes to use when she cuts zigzags in her old blouses, but what im poking around for is a darning needle,

'wheres Mike?' i ask,

and Mums up and powdering her face at the dressing-table mirror,

'dont worry me, darling' she says 'just go and look for him'

i tiptoe into the lounge where im going to try out my experiment and hes not here so i get busy, i force the eye-end of the needle into the seat of an easy chair till the point sticks up about half an inch,

'Mike!' i call 'come and explain this!'

and Mike wanders in with a pencil and drawing pad in his hands,

'what? im busy'

'but it wont take a moment' i tell him,

'what?'

'you have to keep watching that spider up there on the picture rail, and then just sit in this chair'

so Mike shuts his pad and rolls his eyes and he does as hes told,

'YOWWW!'

and hes right up in the air with his arms out wide and the pad and pencil go flying,

i make a dash 'help!' for Mums bedroom,

'Mum!' i yell,

'ohh!' she cries and her hands flap and the powder goes everywhere,

so i dive under the bed to keep her between me and the door,

but Mike charges in,

'im going to kill him!'

'out you go! you know ive got a splitting head!' says Mum 'whats the matter with you? oh you boysll be the death of me!'

'but he—' Mike yells,

'out!' Mum screams,

and that stops him,

but im watching from under the bed and what terrifies me is his white face and the tears in his eyes,

its Palm Sunday and Gran wangles things so we can go to church with her and when the organ stops the priest gets up to tell the story of Jesus walking into Jerusalem but ive heard it all before and i already know the donkey is the best part, but the other good thing is that we are given crosses to take away and each cross is made with a dry reed cleverly folded, so we take an extra one for Mum and i show her when we get home and she puts her thriller down to take hold of it,

'how nice, dear' she says,

and i carry mine into the bedroom, but out of the corner of my eye i catch her throwing hers on the fire,

at last its spring and Patterson says i can come back to see my garden and its been ages so i know the whole thing will just be weeds that have to be pulled out,

'im afraid your dad might catch me' i tell him,

'he wont mind' he says,

so i creep in,

Mrs Patterson is at the kitchen window and she waves to us and she looks the same as before but the window is open,

'do you boys want a glass of lemonade?' she says,

so im wondering if Patterson told a fib, because i cant hear a baby crying and his mother even comes out with the drinks and some scones and jam, and her fingernails are all cracked and her spectacles are dirty,

'did *you* plant these lupins?' she asks me,

and now i see them for the first time and there are three plants with flowers and one with no flowers and everything is looked after, 'yes' i say 'im sorry'

because i can see that Pattersons marrows are already big as sausages,

'the flowers are so pretty' she says 'you must pick one for your mother'

and i dont know what to say,

'take her the blue one' Pattersons mum says 'and leave the pink ones here for me so i can see them when im washing the dishes'

and i pop a scone in my mouth,

she says 'thats my homemade strawberry jam' and she pats my head,

and lupins are my favourite,

i go in to see Mum in the bedroom but the curtains are drawn and shes lying down so i give her the blue lupin and she opens her eyes to look,

'where did this come from?' she says,

but i cant tell her the truth in case she makes me take it back, or even worse she may go round to talk to Mrs Patterson and then she will see their place for herself and their bathtub on the wall and she wont let me go there to play,

'its a lupin' i tell her,

but she doesnt take it and instead she holds her face

in both hands and i watch her lips,

'youll be the death of me' she says '*when* will you boys stop stealing things?'

so i stay there by her bed holding my lupin and waiting to see what she will say next,

but she doesnt say anything,

'then can *i* keep it?' i ask,

and now she digs her fingers into her hair,

'i suppose the damage is done' she says,

in the middle of the night im woken by such golden light that i cant believe what im seeing because the walls are glowing and the cupboard is glowing and shadows flutter like big wings across our room and everything leaps around, so i wake up properly and kneel on the bed to look out the window where a sheet of flame swishes across the black sky and someone thumps at our back door and voices are shouting and i can hear Mum cough while shes on her way to answer it and next thing Mikes standing stiff beside his bed and huge strangers come barging in and one of them grabs his hand to hoist him out,

'hey!' i yell,

and i dive under the bedclothes to hide,

but some other man snatches me up, blankets and all, and gets me and carries me though i struggle like mad but i cant stop him and the whole house is full of men and its too late to scream and in the kitchen one of them has Diana up in his arms while she kicks her legs and Mums there too looking desperate while she buttons up her dressing-gown, so the strangers run through our flat hurling things out of their way like chairs and slamming the doors open, and they never say a word but the whole place is full of their swishing coats and thudding boots and a wind blowing a gale through the house,

'its alright, darlings' Mum says 'these are kind men'

so now i know we are being rescued after all,

the man carrying me joggles me when he stumbles and hes holding too hard and it hurts my ribs and a large black hand swoops across so i cant see,

'what is it?' i yell,

the cold air grabs my feet and now my ears are cold and the wind in the sky is filled with flames,

'what is it?' i yell,

our rescuers crowd in the yard because they dont know where they are or which way to run or escape so they bump against the walls to hurry us through the night past the skylight where i once cut my tongue and now im being carried i look down seeing the skylight glass shine red while above me a fountain of sparks rushes up high above the roof of the covered stairway,

'has something happened?' i say because im not so afraid now, ‘the Gerries hit the shed out the back’ says the man ‘bullseye with an incendiary’

he is rough and smelly and downstairs we plunge inside the sloping tunnel of corrugated iron and im scared he might trip and drop me so i clutch at my trailing blanket to help, but worst is the whole place is chock full of heat so hot i cant breathe, down, down we bump and stumble while Mums calling out the whole time telling us we are going to be safe, and we burst through the bottom door into the lane flying through the air where the night roars and embers swirl and flaming bits of wood patter on the ground and one lump races over like a comet and my man comes to a stop, so i look at his face and there are flames behind his head and behind his bristly hair and he turns his head on his neck and his necks all bristly and he shouts and the flames glint on his teeth and fill his open mouth and then he looks down at me with tiny flames in his eyes,

he says ‘you okay, son?’

the old brick shed is whats been hit because we come to it and watch the flames gushing out and i remember a bird we once found there floating in an open drum of oil with its wings spread, and a cloud of thick smoke leans away over the railway lines and the heat whacks us, so my rescuer grabs a corner of my blanket to cover his head and i cover mine and he makes a dash for it because he has to rush me along scraping me against the brick wall and i catch a glimpse of Diana up ahead in the arms of her man already jogging around the corner and safely away, and now we are in the open street and all this light is the same glare in the shop windows,

'whooo!' and 'blimey!' the rescuers gasp and they let out whistles.

and Mike lets out a whistle just the same,

and i count six and theyre all still choking on smoke and brick dust but some of them begin to laugh and this is so amazingly stupid and theres an old woman with us too, though i dont know how she thought she would help so maybe she just wanted to poke her nose into our flat,

'sorry, old son' says the man carrying me 'did i squash you back there?'

and hes panting,

what i can see is some wooden chairs standing out on the pavement in front of the fish shop where they are not supposed to be and i get put down on one, and the men stand round with their hands on their hips or slapping the embers that glow on their sleeves and Mum sits near me and we watch them stamp their boots and their faces are still bright with the glare from the fire,

'and this is my first night home on leave!' my rescuer tells his friends,

so hes a soldier in civvies! that explains it!

now Di comes over to me and gets up on my chair

too and we huddle together while we listen, all the while looking back the way weve come,

'me and my wife had just got going' he adds 'after being that long separate and *bingo* the fire alarm goes off and all'

others come up and pat him on the back and grin in his face and shake his hand, but he doesnt ever say where he got going *to*,

'are you alright, darlings?' Mum says and shes shivering in her dressing-gown,

'yes, Mum' we say,

and someone lights up a cigarette and the burning shed keeps roaring and popping and crackling and now we see searchlights like fingers in the sky and the fire brigade arrives with men in helmets and uniforms that drag long hoses, and a lady with her hair in curlers is sobbing and reaching out to take hold of Mum,

'good night and thank you' Mum says getting out from between her arms,

and even when we go sloshing back in along the lane when the flames have been put out im still frightened by the smoke,

'are we snobs?' Michael asks on our way upstairs,

'no, darling' Mum says 'snobs are people without refinement'

we all stand in a patch of sun looking at the burnt-out shed that belonged to the garage but now it has no roof and its full of lumps of charcoal as big as trees,

'incendiary bombs' Mike explains to me 'are small lightweight bombs, because the idea is to start fires rather than blow things up'

theres a cleaning lady and her name is Mrs Beckett but she tells us to call her Becky now shes started coming to clean our place for one hour a week and she smiles at me so i see her broken teeth and then she rolls up her sleeves like a workman and gets down on her hands and knees with a stiff brush to brush the carpet, and she does whole rooms like this though i tell her the flats already clean because we cleaned it last Saturday still i have to admit she gets up lots of stuff i didnt know was there that she sweeps into a dustpan and then takes out to the bin, and she whacks the furniture and scrubs the bathroom, and shes an old woman with horrid stringy arms and i hate looking at her when shes working but i cant help myself,

lupins dont last long and my pink ones are finished too and i watch them die and i watch them shrivel up, but i still havent tried out Pattersons bike, and i dont play with him much at school because hes got other friends, and i dont know whats gone wrong,

'hey, Allan' i call,

'Patterson to you' he says,

Mabels here and playing whist with Mum and theyve put up the card table with folding legs and theres two other friends of Mums and theyve all got their elbows on the green top and they smoke and drink beer from our tall glasses and while im colouring in i listen just because thats what i generally do,

'you and your singing, Dods!' says one with her back to me,

'to think i turned down a contract with the Transatlantic Opera Company!' Mum says 'those were the days'

and Mabel says 'who are they, dear?'

'they tour between South Africa and South America' says Mum,

'that sounds exciting'

and i get busy with green to colour in some trees,

'though i took the Birmingham offer instead' Mum says 'because Dick was there'

'so you never thought of going back to the stage' says Mabel 'after?'

Mum shrugs her shoulders,
'with three children?' she says,
'we are going to live in Australia' i tell them,
and they all turn to look at me,
'after' i explain,

halfway down to the canal we stop at the old house that was bombed out at the beginning of the war to see what we can find in the rubble though the front of the house is just a heap of old bricks and you have to poke around and we dig out a broken doll and a rusty pair of scissors, but yesterday Pam told me she found a watch in this ruin, the lucky thing, though it didnt work, but it was a mans watch so thats why i wanted to get it off her.

suddenly everybody is out in the street and *kissing* everybody, all the doors are open and flags hang out of the upstairs windows and Mrs Harris is walking with Gran while church bells on the radio ring out and you can hear them from the open windows of offices and shops and now the real bells of our church begin to ring too swinging up in the steeple, and we all walk around with nowhere to go and even Mr Higgins rushes out of his shoe shop and Roger Sawyers father starts *crying* for goodness sake, and here comes Olive wearing her goggles looking hot and bothered with her horrible mother hobbling along behind,

'its Olive' i shout,

and straight away Olive comes up to hug me and she wont let go because she has to keep showing me how happy she is and her face is all messy with tears,

'weve won the war!' she keeps saying 'weve won the war!'

and i know that already of course,

'*now* will Uncle Ralph come back?' i ask,

'oh, but your Uncle Ralph has forgotten about me!' Olive wails,

'no he hasnt' i say,

but Mum gives me a LOOK,

'i shall be taking the children up to London to see the victory parade' Mum tells Olive 'as soon as we know when its going to be'

but now Olives mother Mrs Freestone catches us up,

'good afternoon, Mrs Freestone' i say,

'is *that* child here?' says Mrs Freestone,

and a whole lot of cheering begins but its nothing to do with us,

'the children are going to have a treat' Olive tells her mother 'because Dods is going to take them to see the king' 'what they deserve is spanked bottoms if you ask me' says Mrs Freestone,

but Mum gives her a kiss on the cheek just the same and suddenly shes smiling too and thats amazing because it cracks her face open,

'we shall have to find out when its going to be' Mum says 'but itll give them something to remember for the rest of their lives because therell never be another victory parade like this'

'*some* of us remember the last one!' says Mrs Freestone,

and she blows her nose loud as a fart,

'hip hip hooray!' call a whole lot of voices down near the railway station,

but i cant see whats happening there,

'theres an eleven forty pm to London' Mike tells Mum,

'at *night*?' Mrs Freestone says 'i never heard of such a thing'

'nor me' i say,

'well we shall need to arrive in London nice and early in the morning to get a good position to see' says Mum,

and an old guy with dribble on his chin reaches out to shake hands with me, though i dont like touching his bent old hand or looking at his bent old back and he shakes Mikes hand too and he pats Di on the head and his backs bent, because we know that what hes got is sleepy sickness and we sometimes see him reading a book in the bus shelter but here he is out in the street propped up on his walking sticks and he looks *disgusting*, and now theres a whole lot of clapping because the nurses are wheeling some wounded soldiers down from the hospital and everybody stands back to let them through,

'peace!' Mrs Harris shouts 'peace at last!'

Olives mothers grey hair sticks out everywhere 'but you can bet we havent seen the end of *rationing*' she says,

'cheer up, Mrs Freestone' says Mrs Harris,

'well i know wholl have the last laugh' Mrs Freestone says,

and Grans hand in a grey glove covers her mouth and the glove has a button at the wrist,

'as long as someone *does* laugh' says Mrs Harris,

'we must send a telegram to Uncle Mont' Mum says,

so I take hold of Olives hand,

'and Uncle Ralph too' i say,

'dont mention that man in my hearing' says Mrs Freestone,

and a whole lot of women come skipping arm-in-arm till the whole streets full of them and theyre dressed in red-white-and-blue and silly hats and in among them Mabel Greenwood is waving to us, and everybody joins in the noise and the dancing when an old gypsy wanders around playing a squeeze-box and Mrs Harris shows us how to tap our feet in time and shes so big she looks silly but we have to clear off the road anyhow to let the Home Guard through because theyre marching in a procession wearing badges and Allan Pattersons right at the front with his dad and the fire brigades behind them and there are two policemen wheeling bikes,

'is this the victory parade?' i ask,

'well its the best this miserable town can do' Mrs Freestone says,

'just wait till we get to London, next week' Mum says to me 'then youll see!'

and now the town is full of men in uniform getting off trains and out of buses and lorries and some go straight into Mrs Harrises pub and Allan Pattersons dads with them, and Allan and some other boys sit on the steps outside and theyre drinking orangeade, so i go up to see,

'is that orangeade?' i say,

but i know Patterson is not my friend now,

'my Uncle Franks back from the war' he tells me all the same,

'is that good, then?' i ask,

'i dont know' Patterson says 'but hes in there with Dad'

and one of the boys shifts his bottom to give me room

to sit down with them,

'anyway he gave me a real sheath knife'

'cor!' says a boy behind us,

'you lucky thing!' i say,

'but dad hit me' Patterson says,

'like smacked?' says the boy behind 'or punched?'

'smacked'

'did it hurt?' i say,

'it hurt' Patterson says 'like a bugger'

'did you cry?' i whisper so the others cant hear,

'shove off!' Patterson shouts at me,

and i explain,

'well my Uncle Ken is in the army and once he came home on leave and he hit my sister and now *hes* come back home too and hes a captain and he gave my cousin a toy clown that you can bend into any shape thats called Twerpy'

'why Twerpy?'

'because it got bought somewhere called Antwerpy'

'wheres that?'

'i dunno' i say 'unless its at the frontline'

and the doors burst open behind us so we all skip out of the way while the men come out but Mr Patterson gets hold of Pattersons ear and twists it,

'this is my brat' he says,

and the men look down at Patterson but one of them goes to the gutter to spew, 'kids never grow up fast enough' he says, shaking drops from his mouth,

every time someone toots a horn down in the street i rush to the window to see if its Uncle Ralph and we know he came home last week because he walked into our bedroom just when i was going to sleep and ruffled my hair but in the morning he was gone and im on the lookout for his sports car again because i forgot to ask him if he ever got my envelope that i printed, and im kneeling on the settee looking out of the window and calling to Mum though something seems to have gone wrong, and Mum comes in and shes crying,

'get yourself dressed in your Sunday best' she tells me, something awfuls happened,

'this is *Saturday*' i remind her,

'Mum!' says Diana, running at her,

but Mum turns her back,

'put your blue frock on' she tells Di and pushes her away,

and i dont know whats the matter,

'wheres Mike?' i ask,

'hes on an errand for me' Mum says looking grim,

and she puts her hat on while she goes to the back door where she sticks a hatpin into it, ‘youre to walk to Grans place when youre ready’ Mum tells us ‘and make sure you lock the house first’ and she opens the door ‘i will be there as soon as i can’

and shes gone,

‘whats up, Rod?’ Di whispers,

but i just dip my comb in the washbasin and comb my hair down flat with a proper parting on the left,

and Dis plaits are already done so all she needs to do is button up her shoes and we can be off,

‘wheres Mike *gone*?’ i say,

‘it must be bad’ Di says,

and it is, because the fish lady goes quiet when she sees us dressed up on the wrong day and Mr Sawyer takes off his hat and when we get to Grans place it looks strange because the front windows are open and some curtains puff out and the front doors not shut,

‘what i reckon is that Grans dead’ i whisper to Di ‘because shes so old’

and Di looks scared,

‘but i wanted to tell her’ she says ‘we are going to London for the victory parade’

and we open the garden gate but we dont like to step indoors because already the house smells like disinfectant so we hang around among the peonies,

‘look!’ says Di,

and she runs squealing out into the street and already shes hugging Gran whos wearing a black dress with purple buttonholes and on her way in, so Gran stops to kiss us but her nose is red and her eyes are watery and she rocks when she walks and i rock from one leg to the other to be like her, and now i know the reason she does it is to feel good, and she goes in with us but she closes her front room on the way,

'youre not to go there' she says,

and Joan and Ken and Olive are already sitting round Grans kitchen table and Olive has her face stuck in a big handkerchief,

but suddenly theres the sound of a door opening and that gets Gran going so shes sobbing out loud and i peep down the passageway and its only Mum and Michael but theyre bringing Doctor Halliday with his hat held against his chest, and Mike looks serious about something so i wish i could go into the front room too, but Olive tucks her hanky away and reaches up and wraps her arms around me and she hangs on to me because im her favourite and shes got hiccups,

'its Uncle Ralph' i say out loud, and Doctor Halliday comes out

'he looks peaceful' he tells us,

and puts his hat on and Mum shows him to the front door,

and thats when Diana bursts out howling and now Olive looks up at me, so im trying to believe Uncle Ralph is really dead and im trying to cry, ‘its a tragedy’ Ken says ‘he was still in his prime’

and i keep trying but the tears wont come and i dont know whats the matter with me and i dont know what to feel because i dont feel anything at all, and now Gran comes back to the kitchen to fill the kettle,

‘but all he did’ Olive wails in a loud voice ‘was go to the cinema!’

‘he was standing right outside’ says Gran,

and Ken puts his arm around Joan because shes his wife and shes holding baby Andrew in her arms so she cant do anything except cry,

‘nevertheless’ Ken says ‘it was a good clean way to go’

‘he just dropped dead on the spot’ says Olive ‘apparently’

but all the women are around us and watching us and crying while they are telling us about it and Mikes crying too, so i know i have to do my bit and i know what they expect and im usually such a good liar, but its no good,

and now Mums looking at me so she can see im not sorry and she thinks i dont care,

‘Rod’ she asks me ‘are you remembering the white feather?’

this is such a brilliant idea that i nod,

‘i thought so’ she says,

and kisses me,

‘what white feather?’ Ken booms,

Diana takes hold of my hand,

but now Mums squatting down so she can look at us both on the level,

'darlings' she explains 'theres something you should know about your Uncle Ralph'

Olive lets out a sob,

'while the war was on he had to keep a secret' Mum says 'none of us knew, not even Gran'

'*none* of us' Olive wails,

'because hed been sworn to secrecy' Mum says 'and Gran and Joan and i, well we worried about that and we suffered'

Di and i look at one another because we dont know what to do, and the kettle starts singing on the stove,

'we kept wishing he would enlist even though he was his age' Mum weeps 'well, now we know'

'he *did*!' Gran pipes up,

and i dont know if theres more to come or if thats it,

'no reason to be ashamed of old Ralph' says Ken,

'poor Ralph' says Joan, stroking her babys head,

'and now, so we hear' Mum says 'theres a citation'

at last i can stop pretending,

'whats a citation?' i ask,

'a kind of medal' Michael tells me,

'from the Special Air Service Regiment' Gran says,

she takes down a tea caddy and she sets out some cups and saucers, and Olive gets up to fetch a bottle of milk from the pantry and pours some into a jug and covers it with a little fly net so the fringe beads tinkle against the china,

'it turns out that all this time' Mum says 'hes been on active service in the Air Force'

'right from the beginning of the war' Gran says,

'no one knew' Olive wails,

and Ken pats his moustache,

'all he ever told me' Gran says 'was that he trained recruits'

'your Uncle Ralph was a glider pilot' Ken tells us,

'i think of him out there at night' Mum says 'gliding high above enemy territory on a secret mission'

'with paratroopers aboard' Joan says at last 'all ready to jump out over enemy territory'

'my brother Ralph' says Mum,

now i can see him too and i can see his glider gliding in the dark air and the aerofoils lifting him and i can see those paratroopers getting ready to jump,

'so its a mystery that his heart gave out when it did' Gran says 'back home safe and sound and taking himself to the pictures'

'just like that' Ken says and snaps his fingers,

Uncle Ralph is dead and Mums given me his sunglasses to keep for a week, and she found a lost photo of *you* and im going to keep looking at it because i never knew you smoked a white pipe in an army camp, and im going to drink a bottle of beer too when i grow up,

The things on Grans table are not much, just a badge thats two golden wings and a propelling pencil made of silver and a mans wallet and stuff, a few letters and a postcard on top addressed to Mr Ralph Buckland with a small red Edward VIII penny stamp like the ones ive got in my album,

Dear old chap

Dods brought the baby to visit me. The little fellow has inherited such lung power from someone in the family he bawled and bawled the whole time! Operatic, to put it mildly. But it did my heart good to hear him. And my little girl is growing into such a darling she's the image of my sister Gertrude. And young Michael is a proper trooper, I'm proud to say. After they left I waved to them from the window and Dods held the baby up for a last look. Well, life in a hospital is not something I'd recommend. Stay out of it as long as you can. So happy about your visit too, it was a proper tonic*. Thanks for coming,*

Dick

Acknowledgements & Notes

Shortly before Joan's death in July 2006 I was grateful to have the chance of sharing these memories with her ... and, of course, with Michael and Diana, without whom very little of this would have happened in the first place. I have written everything down, exactly as I remember it, for my family—for Bet and our darling daughters, Imogen, Delia and Cressida—and for theirs.

My objective is to recapture each incident as it was stamped on my memory at the time: necessarily, this entails reconstructing dialogue true to the accent and character of the speakers—as legitimate a part of memory as the incidents themselves. I am grateful to Dylan Clau whose fine ear for nuance has been of great assistance in my rediscovery of the child's own voice.

Thanks are also due to my publisher, Colette Vella, my agent, Mary Cunnane, and to the wonderful people at Victoria University, Elizabeth Harman, John McCallum and all.

p.51 coms. Short for combinations. This was an old-fashioned full-length undergarment combining vest and pants, covering the whole body from neck to ankle, sometimes with long sleeves too.

p.65 indelible pencil. Obsolete now though, at the time, every child knew what an indelible pencil was and that you couldn't rub out what you had written if you used one, also that the sharpened lead would stain your tongue purple if you licked it.

p.274 Percy Edgar (Dick) Hall enlisted as private soldier No.415, 'C' Company, the Prince of Wales' Own Regiment [front row, left]. Photograph taken at Colsterdale camp, Yorkshire circa 1914.

Published in 2010 by Pier 9, an imprint of Murdoch Books Pty Limited

Murdoch Books Australia
Pier 8/9
23 Hickson Road
Millers Point NSW 2000
Phone: +61 (0) 2 8220 2000
Fax: +61 (0) 2 8220 2558
www.murdochbooks.com.au

Murdoch Books UK Limited
Erico House, 6th Floor
93–99 Upper Richmond Road
Putney, London SW15 2TG
Phone: +44 (0) 20 8785 5995
Fax: +44 (0) 20 8785 5985
www.murdochbooks.co.uk

Publisher: Colette Vella
Project Editor: Kate Fitzgerald
Designer: Sandy Cull

National Library of Australia Cataloguing-in-Publication Data
Author: Hall, Rodney
Title: Popeye Never Told You, childhood memories of the war / Rodney Hall.
ISBN: 9781741967593 (hbk.)
Subjects: Hall, Rodney, 1935---Childhood and youth. World War, 1939-1945--Children--England--Biography--Anecdotes World War, 1939-1945--Children--England--Social conditions. Children and war --England--Biography--Anecdotes
Dewey Number: A823.3

PRINTED IN CHINA.